TESTAMENT FROM A PRISON CELL

TESTAMENT
FROM A
PRISON CELL

By

BENIGNO S. AQUINO, JR.

Published by the PHILIPPINE JOURNAL, INC.
LOS ANGELES, CALIFORNIA, U.S.A.

Published, with written permission, by the PHILIPPINE JOURNAL, INC.
for the benefit of the BENIGNO S. AQUINO, JR. FOUNDATION

PUBLISHER: MARIO Ca. FERNANDEZ
EDITORS: CONSUELO G. FERNANDEZ
        MARK G. DE VERA
        ED LEONCIO
        ART PALALAY
DESIGNS: CHARLES O. FUNK, ARNOLD ADAO
FIRST PRINTING IN THE U.S.A.
LIMITED EDITION

You have been told, O man,
what is good, and what the Lord
requires of you: only this,
to act justly,
to love mercy,
and to walk humbly with your God.

MICAH 6:8

TABLE OF CONTENTS

LIST OF PHOTOS

Prologue

At 10:25 p.m. on November 25, 1977, Benigno S. Aquino, Jr. and his two co-accused, Bernabe Buscayno and Lt. Victor Corpuz, were sentenced to death by firing squad by Philippine Military Commission No. 2.

Immediately after he was returned to his cell, Aquino wrote a six-page letter to the justices of the Supreme Court in which he described in detail what happened during the thirteen hours that led to the military's Black Friday Night decision.

He called it "an infamous rush to judgment."

"I was deceitfully silenced and effectively prevented from availing myself of the various options open to me under the Manual of Court Martial by the simple expedient of keeping me locked in my cell during the vital eight hours of the proceedings," Aquino wrote the Supreme Court.

Specifically, Aquino told the Court he was not allowed to read his statement before judgment—"my right," he pointed out, as provided in Sec. 76 of the Manual of Court Martial.

This is the statement the Military Commission prevented Aquino from reading in open court.

In this statement, Aquino explains the meaning of his obstinate struggle, his ideology and his proposed strategy for national survival. He seeks to focus the attention of the Filipino people and the world on the wanton violations of human rights by the martial law administrators. He identifies the victims of torture and their torturers, and reveals the torture methods used by Marcos' military investigators. By citing case after appalling case, he describes how detainees have been framed with confessions brutally tortured out of them—and how others, especially Marcos' uncompromising political enemies, are framed with similarly secured confessions.

It is Aquino's most powerful indictment of the Marcos dictatorship which held him prisoner for more than seven years.

As to the sentence meted him—death by musketry—his statement shows that he expected it. That he was prepared for it. Indeed, as he had repeatedly stated: "I would rather die on my feet with honor, than live on bended knees in shame."

On August 27, 1973, Aquino had served notice to the Military Commission that he would not defend himself. For by defending himself, he said, he would lend credibility to a "kangaroo court." But he reserved the right to read this statement, which he wrote under the most trying circumstances in his maximum-security prison cell in Camp Bonifacio.

The Military Commission must have considered this statement so explosive that to prevent its being read in open court, it chose to ignore the guarantees of due process and violate Aquino's constitutional rights. Aquino's "testament from a prison cell" is indeed a document to be feared and suppressed—by those who are afraid of the truth, and the eventual triumph of truth, justice, democracy and freedom.

FOREWORD

This book is Ninoy's "closing statement" before Military Commission No. 2.

Ninoy started working on his "closing statement" in 1975 and he finished it in 1977. Although many believed that the charges against him were fabricated, still Ninoy believed he should present his side to the Filipino people.

Ninoy was determined that this book should reach his people and so my children and I smuggled out the manuscript, page by page. He instructed me to furnish the international press with copies of his statement. Perhaps he had a premonition. As it turned out, the Military Commission prevented Ninoy from reading from his "closing statement" by keeping him locked up in his cell during the last vital eight hours of the proceedings.

I cannot help but point out the striking parallel between Ninoy's closing statement before the tribunal that condemned him to death on November 25, 1977, and his "arrival statement" for August 21, 1983. In both instances Ninoy was stopped from reading them.

Allow me then to present to you, the Filipino people, Ninoy's testament.

Cory Aquino

INTRODUCTION

T he cry of protest of a newborn child is the first sign of life. So also are the fearless protests of citizens a testimony to the vibrant health of a democracy.

Through the ages, it has been the protest of man against the vagaries of nature, against the cruelties of his environment, and against the tyranny of his governors that has lifted him from his primal animal origins to his present civilization.

Protest is part and parcel of the democratic evolution of man. And democracy is enlarged and strengthened, rather than eroded and weakened, by conflict and dissent.

Indeed, as Senator J. William Fulbright stressed in *The Arrogance of Power:*

> In a democracy dissent is an act of faith. Like medicine, the test of its value is not its taste but its effect, not how it makes people feel at the moment but how it makes them feel and moves them to act in the long run. Criticism may embarrass the country's leaders in the short run but strengthen their hand in the long run...Criticism, in short, is more than a right; it is an act of patriotism, a higher form of patriotism, I believe, than the familiar rituals of national adulation.

"The unexamined life," said Socrates in an ancient Greece, "is not worth living."

To a citizen of democracy, to protest is not only a right, it is a duty and it imposes an obligation on the government to listen, to consider and to be guided by what the community says.

It was with this philosophy of the democratic man that I served our people in the Philippine Senate, seeking only the truth and fearing nothing — neither the truth nor any man. It is the same public philosophy I have abided by unflinchingly since the seizure of absolute power by Mr. Marcos.

Thus, since September 23, 1972, when I was among the very first to be arrested and held in military detention, I have protested the one-man rule Mr. Marcos has instituted, which has stifled our democracy and established a totalitarian regime in our beloved Filipinas.

Over the last five years I have protested against a system that arrogates to one man the absolute power to be *the* accuser, *the* prosecutor and *the* judge of his own accusations. And in my unique case, it is even worse: because the man is my personal political adversary, whose presidency I have zealously fiscalized.

Over the last five years, I have protested the trial of civilians by Mr. Marcos' military tribunals while all our civil courts are functioning and have never ceased to function. Military tribunals are institutions for discipline, not justice — courts of convenience, not courts of justice. Mr. Marcos exercises not only *command influence* but absolute *command control* over these tribunals. His is always the last word!

It was with this blatant injustice in mind — to set my position in fullest perspective — that I declared on August 27, 1973, that I would not participate in the proceedings of a military tribunal whose members are all subordinate officers to a "President" who, a year before his imposition of martial rule, already pronounced me guilty, on national television, of almost the same charges I was now to be tried for. Mr. Marcos did not file any of his charges — not one! — against me with the civil courts in 1971. Why? Because, as I have repeatedly pointed out, the civil courts were not then under his control.

Mr. Marcos charged me only eleven months after he had created the military tribunals whose members are all appointed by him, who are all under his absolute command as martial law authority, who may be replaced any time at his pleasure, and whose findings are merely recommendatory, subject to his personal review and final decision. I find this not only grossly anomalous, immoral, unjust and unjustified — but an unconscionable mockery of justice, an obscene farce!

On that August day in 1973, I told Mr. Marcos' military tribunal that I would not defend myself, that I fully realized the consequences of my decision, that I had chosen to obey my conscience whatever the tyrant's verdict. To have done otherwise, to have traded what is right for my accommodation, I held, would have done violence to all I have ever stood for. I reiterate this position today, more firmly than on the day I first made it.

I do not fear to appear before the bar of justice. But give me a court of disinterested, independent and humane men, not a tribunal under the orders of my accuser. Back in 1971, I challenged Mr. Marcos to bring me to court — "there to be exposed who is lying, he or I." He did not take up my challenge.

So, my decision remains unchanged — not to participate; let the tyrant do as he wishes with me.

I indulge in no vain hopes: he has wanted to have either my fealty or my head.

So, as I have said in the past, I yield my body to Mr. Marcos. It is the highest privilege, my last act of freedom, to choose to die at the dictator's hands, before the eyes of our people and all humanity, rather than live on my bended knees at the feet of tyranny.

But at the moment when the bullets of his musketry rip my body and take my life, let him be asked: What was Aquino's crime?

Yes, what is my crime? I say: None, except to have stood up to Mr. Marcos, to have unmasked his sinister designs on our Republic, to have exposed the evil, predatory ways of his mis-government.

The ironies are too harsh and the tragedy too profound to be overlooked. But

I take a certain consolation in my fate: It exposes to the whole world the sad situation of our people. It shows where we are, with Mr. Marcos' seizure of absolute power: a throwback to rule by the Lord of the Manor.

This is tyranny at its worst, where men are at the absolute disposal of their governor — to be kept alive, if the governor chooses, or to be killed, if the governor so desires.

No amount of cosmetics can doll up his dictatorship. It will be there nakedly exposed, before the civilized world.

My fate also shows our people what they have become — a people desensitized by Marcos' rule by fear — and what they can still be. In this way, I hope to regenerate their capacity for indignation, revive the functions of their individual consciences, and restore their ability to dream once more, not only of a greater measure of freedom, but of a life that is truly free.

The worst thing Mr. Marcos has done to our people is to devalue their human values and habituate them to this. He has made conformity the highest value. He has deformed our people's sense of self-dignity and cheapened their self-worth. The net effect has been to disfigure the national psyche, with this sorry result: a people truculent within, obedient without.

"The regime of fear produces dreaming and servile races," Walter Lippmann wrote. But beyond this, he hastened to point out, is the greater damage to the nation by what it does to "those who are yet to be born." He elucidated, taking up the Nazi philosophy as a case in point:

> All Germans must sink into docile but eager resignation, accepting the decisions of the Fuehrer as the fellah accepts the will of Allah; and then out of this conforming mass must arise brilliant, adventurous, and supremely intelligent leaders...A population is dogmatically drilled, its curiosity is frustrated, it is forbidden to examine the premises or conclusion of the official dogma, it is unable to exchange ideas at home or abroad — and then it is called upon to produce leaders. This is the most puzzling paradox of the Nazi philosophy. For the principle of leadership is highly individualistic. It presupposes the continual emergence of resourceful men; but the principle of absolute collective conformity from birth to death would hardly seem calculated to develop and select them.
>
> It is easy enough to understand how temporarily convenient the paradox is to the prevailing dictators. The principle of leadership justifies their own arbitrary powers and the principle of obedient conformity justifies their denial of power to anyone else. But since, according to Hitler's own assurances, National Socialism is to last for a thousand years, the problem of how new leaders are to be recruited is a serious one for those who take seriously the aspirations of the Nazis.

Yes, Filipinos are oppressed and driven by fear — fear for self, fear for family; fear of Marcos and his "Brown Shirts"!

The fateful question I have asked myself endlessly: Is this our destiny as a people? And always the answer I get: No, it cannot be. It must not be!

My deepest concern, my fondest wish, therefore, is to see democracy restored in our benighted land, with our public life regenerated by self-correction and self-renewal. And I see this coming even now: Our people, even as they are whipsawed from fear to tears and back, yearn to be free, hunger for liberty.

It has been a long night. But it will end.

Leadership, especially in times of evil rule or evil threat, exacts a harsh price — a price that, if the leader be true, he can only meet gladly, accept unreservedly and pay willingly. Of such mold were the men Winston Churchill forged into England's War Cabinet, who, after Dunkirk, "were each ready to be killed quite soon, and have all his family and possessions destroyed, rather than give in." Ghosts of such men have been my cellmates in my solitary prison cell. They inspire me to be ever faithful to country and duty.

According to Sigmund Freud, men may be divided into the leaders and the led. The led need a high command to make decisions for them — "to which decision they usually bow without demur." The leaders to deserve rank must be independent thinkers, unyielding to intimidation, and fervent in the quest for truth, because their primary role is to guide the led.

I voluntarily sought the role of leader; no one forced me into it. I was barely of legal age when I started in public office. I was barely 35 years old when the Filipino people sent me to the Senate. I gloried in its pomp, and I must now suffer its deprivation.

I was the lone survivor on the Senate opposition ticket in 1967. In that election campaign, where Mr. Marcos used all the powers of the presidency to prevent my election, I pledged to our people that I would be their uncompromising and dedicated watch-dog in government. I fully realized the import of my pledge. I knew even then that someday, if things went from bad to worse, I might end up a martyr to my cause.

Now it has come. But I am determined to persevere till the end. I have no armor to wear, no lance to throw, no sword to wield — indeed, I am in Marcos' prison cell, awaiting the final verdict of Mr. Marcos himself — but I have liberty for my cause, truth for my tool and the last freedom to speak the truth. And, in the words of St. Thomas Aquinas, "to honestly help my fellow men to know what they ought to believe, what they ought to desire, what they ought to do."

It may be shouting at the darkness, as some may say. But then Churchill did "no more than sound the roar" — and see what he achieved!

Is it folly? I think not.

I know it will serve destiny's purpose. As Gandhi said, "The willing sacrifice of the innocent is the most powerful retort to insolent tyranny that has yet been conceived by God or man." To which, in my conscientisized resistance, I add this civil rights axiom from America's black martyr, Martin Luther King: "Freedom is never voluntarily given by the oppressor; it must be demanded by the oppressed."

And the simple fact is: We are a captive people, held captive by a domestic despot.

The most basic of our human rights — those "inherent and inalienable Rights" which, in Thomas Jefferson's words, emanate from "the Laws of Nature and of Nature's God" and are at the heart of the democratic philosophy as "self-evident truths," "the Essence of Man, which is not accidental, which does not go with the passage of time and with the rise and fall of fads and styles and systems" — have been stripped from our people by a leadership that has betrayed its oath "to preserve and defend the Constitution, execute its laws, do justice to every man."

Mr. Marcos himself has specified the extent of the "suspension"- to use the martial law authority's language - of every Filipino's fundamental right guaranteed our people by our Constitution. In his *Notes,* he writes: "Martial law necessarily creates a command society"; "It (the martial regime) will not encroach upon the private lives of all our citizens; in *this space of freedom,* the citizen may behave as he pleases in the pursuit of his private happiness: he may order or disrupt his life according to his discipline or lack of it"; beyond that is the realm of the martial law. (Marcos, *Notes,* Page 80)

Indeed, as Mr. Marcos' own decrees testify, he has taken away from our people their rights to free speech, free press, free assembly, free labor, free vote, free government — and, of course, their freedom from illegal entry into their homes, illegal seizure of their belongings, and illegal arrest of their persons.

By my non-participation, at the cost of my physical freedom and the jeopardy of my beloved wife and children, I hope to arouse the conscience of our people who ultimately can put an end to this nightmare of a dictatorship. They are our country's real and true sovereign.

I have reached my decision in the faith that "right defeated is stronger than evil triumphant."

I believe that to live but a single day in defense of liberty is better than living a hundred years in fear or in the service of tyranny.

And if all be lost for me, then I take solace with the French: "Everything is lost but honor." So be it with me.

BENIGNO S. AQUINO, JR.

I

CLAIMS AND REALITIES

> ...and seek a region more fine, for my
> country vows to give fetters for your
> laurels, a dark jail for your shrine.
>
> — TO MY..., JOSE RIZAL, 1890

IN THESE DARK times, when even the mildest criticism is taken by the powers that be as a form of treason, the pervading atmosphere of fear makes calm thought most difficult. Even a whispered protest calls for a measure of bravery. How much more a defiant cry?

In a "command society," as Mr. Marcos calls his New Society, where "fear" is a key element of rule, it is deemed necessary to defer to the force that is kept poised over your head or be crushed under it. "When *I* use a word, it means just what I choose it to mean — neither more nor less," tells the fearful Alice in Lewis Carroll's *Through the Looking-Glass;* so it is with Mr. Marcos' New Filipinos.

It is a melancholy time in our history — a time when truth is heresy and heresy truth. The truth is mauled, twisted and bent in the pit of tyranny — and the people, told they are on the way to "a greater freedom," accept it mutely and find themselves deeper in slavery.

But how else could they take it?

Martial rule assaults the senses, numbs the mind, drives a sense of overpowering doom into those who would disagree. Fear is the key instrument, as Mr. Marcos has said so cynically — and the people do fear.

It is a time of formidable fears requiring incredible courage of those who would respond heroically to the challenge.

But this is also the time when a summons to do what is right is a summons for men to be like steel, to shed their fears, to sort things out, to recognize their moral duty, and demand what they must: a rule of law, not rule by man, and only one at that; and then their freedom!

I do not claim to be a cut above the common man. Indeed, as I stand here, I am humbled by the shades of the fallen among my beloved Filipinos in their struggles to be free. With head bowed, I say: May I always do as the heritage you have given us bids me; may I never falter in bearing aloft the torch you have passed on to me.

And by the same measure, as I make my "last hurrah" — to borrow the grim gallows humor of the trial counsel — I direct the only plea I am making in this trial to the Filipino people: Having failed to avert our present catastrophe, let us at least learn from it.

Firstly, let us confront and ponder what has so tragically befallen us. And ask ourselves: Why?

The "whys" are simple, painfully so — in retrospect:

— We failed to value our freedom, forgetting that it was won at heroic sacrifice by martyred forebears and must be defended at every turn, lest it be chipped, nibbled at and finally taken away by a clever and conscienceless tyrant;

— We forgot what the epic men of various races and varied times have handed down to us as mankind's eternal truth, that "freedom is indivisible and the rights denied one man is surely the beginning of the denial of the rights of us all";

— We forgot, so ironically, because it is part of our great inheritance, what Rizal told us. "There are no tyrants where there are no slaves," and what earlier Liberty's noble woman, Madame Roland, left as a legacy to all free men as she mounted the guillotine, "Eternal vigilance is the price of liberty!"

The lesson — Liberty's Truth — is: A people that is not willing to speak out for freedom, and to suffer and die for it, does not deserve freedom.

Secondly, we ought now to draw the signal lesson: that a democracy, no matter its imperfections, is still the best government conceived by man and certainly is to be desired over rule by martial law, rule by a dictatorship, rule by a tyrant.

"Government by the consent of the governed is the most difficult system of all because it depends for its success and viability on the good judgment and wise decision of so many of us," wrote Adlai Stevenson, summing up his failed campaign for the U.S. presidency in 1952. But he hastened to add, quoting Thomas Jefferson's letter to John Tyler 150 years before:

> No experiment can be more interesting than that we are now trying, and which we trust will end in establishing the fact that man may be governed by reason and truth...

I hold it, therefore, certain that to open the doors of truth, and to fortify the habit of testing everything by reason, are the most effectual manacles we can rivet on the hands of our successors to prevent their manacling the people with their consent. The panic into which they were artfully thrown in 1798, the frenzy which was excited in them by their enemies against their friends, and their apparent readiness to abandon all the principles established for their own protection, seemed for a while to countenance the opinions of those who say they cannot be trusted with their own government. But I never doubted their rallying; and they did rally much sooner than I expected. On the whole, that experiment on their credulity has confirmed my confidence in their ultimate good sense and virtue.

Absolute power, on the other hand, whether in a king, a president, a protector, a pretender, or a martial law authority, is not only alien to our idea of "democratic decision," but, without fail, gets to be arbitrary and despotic, corrupt and corrupting, unjust and unwise—as now, now that we have lost our democracy, we find to our common sorrow. It is, whatever the icing on it, tyranny.

Through our present sufferings, through the acids of the tyranny, may we rediscover these first and last things again—our freedom and our rights—and be stronger for the ordeal of a renewed commitment to our democratic ideals.

May the Filipinos who survive this native despotism take to heart the lessons that it teaches: that freedom does not come cheap and easy, that dissent is most despised when most needed; that the enemy within is to be feared and could even be more evil and destructive than any foe from the outside.

What if freedom and liberation are not achieved by this generation? I say: There will be other generations. What is vital is that this generation sacrifice its blood and strike a blow for freedom to merit honor and fond remembrance.

In any case, there is nature's law: Despots are human too, and like all human beings subject to decay. When fate beckons, even monarchs must obey. Sooner or later, even the most powerful dictator is called from his throne of power to render an accounting to the God of Justice. It is inevitable that this nightmare will pass.

I am not the only one on trial here. Mr. Marcos, his martial rule and its judicial processes are also at the bar. For every charge hurled against me, Mr. Marcos stands doubly charged!

Mr. Marcos will be judged by the nation he has betrayed and deceived—not only by this generation, but by all generations of Filipinos yet to be born, whenever this dark page in our history is recalled in disgust, in shame, in horror.

Very soon, I will be condemned to obscurity and oblivion. Even now there are massive efforts to re-write our history and to suppress the truth. But as long as there is breath left in me, I shall not be silenced!

Indulge me with your patience and please carefully consider these thoughts:

—*To "save" democracy Mr. Marcos killed it.* Like all other dictators, he invoked the people as rationale for his act. "It is for the people that we embark on the democratic revolution," he writes in *Today's Revolution,* his *Mein Kampf.* "I am utilizing this power vested in me by the Constitution to save the Republic and reform our society."

Mr. Marcos entered it into the records as "Proclamation No. 1081," but he might well have titled it "How to Create a Constitutional Crisis, then Seize Total Power to Resolve It." It was, as he admits in the preface to his *Notes on the New Society,* an act that had absorbed him for some time, that he had planned and executed finally as a "historical necessity." What he inadvertently revealed in his arrogance was that martial rule was a premeditated plan.

This, against all his pious avowals that he would never impose martial law. He would not put Filipino constitutionality in jeopardy, he had told the people repeatedly, even if the youth and rebels imperilled his life. But now he told a different tale: "The thrust of history, and even the will of the people, somehow guided my hand to the deed. By a single act, it was done."

It was done, indeed. "By a single-act," coupled with the stern threat of "death by musketry" for those who dared oppose him, he raped liberty in liberty's name, killed freedom allegedly for freedom's safety, and interred democracy in a squalid grave to, in his words, "save democracy."

—*Mr. Marcos claims to have established a New Society.* What we really have is the oldest society known to man, one that dates back to the divine right of kings when one man ruled and his will was the Law, his person the State.

—*Mr. Marcos promised the Filipinos a society in "greater freedom."* But today, five years after he imposed martial law and launched his New Society, what we have is a *society in fear.* Fear, he has said, is an instrument of his martial rule.

Fear has been the pervasive presence in our people's lives since the Marcos *golpe* fell. "Prudence is the better part of valor" became the counsel in many a Filipino home. *"Sumayaw sa banda* (dance with the band)," as one erstwhile political leader told his family. Only in a few did courage combine with outrage to produce action, no matter how disorganized. The great many balked: they were furious, but they were weak; who were they to pit themselves against the dictator and his minions?

In fairness to the Filipinos, it was a primal reaction, of which almost all peoples share a common historical guilt. In the mid-July 1942 round-up of French Jews by the Gestapo, for example, the compassion and desire to help wilted—"aborted by fear," in the account I read—in many a Frenchman. "It is," as a psychologist wrote, "a behavior that makes them like all humanity, neither better nor worse when confronted by a crisis of conscience." This is one of the tragedies of existence.

In this, Mr. Marcos has shrewdly taken the Filipinos' measure. He made his calculations well, as he later all but trumpeted: when he let the ax drop, the people would be too stricken with fear to resist. They would think only of their safety and become completely apathetic.

— *Ours, Mr. Marcos says, is "a parliamentary form of government."* But as *Newsweek* correctly observed, ours is the only parliamentary government in the world "without a parliament." His "parliament" was, first, his *barangays* and now his *sanggunians*. To call these a parliament is a preposterous doctrine, a sophistry: this is a travesty of representative government, the supreme heresy of our time!

What happened to our Congress was atrocious. Congress, sacred house of Filipino government, was literally invaded and padlocked by the PC-Metrocom while it was on *sine die*, an act equalled in its brazenness only by Napoleon's dispatch of troops into the Chamber of Deputies and Cromwell's military occupation of Parliament. The people's representatives had stood there as sentinels and brakes against executive despotism since the Commonwealth years; it was now, in the poignant lament of one of its elders, "put to the sword." He would, Mr. Marcos proclaimed, henceforth legislate by fiat.

Much besides died with the Philippine Congress. Not just the mechanism that exposed the follies of Philippine presidents, not merely a school for leaders in the art of government, nor only occasional circuses some of its members had provided the laughing galleries—one of its failings. More than this, Congress had been the free and unfettered chamber of the people. Congress provided the necessary checks and balances, consultations and accountability, the control on the purse as a counterpoise to the power of the sword, taxation only with representation, and representation only by the people's free vote.

Now, by his "single act," Mr. Marcos did away with all of these. Nobody was left to check him or balance his power. He was accountable to none. And whenever he pleased he could tax, as he indeed has taxed, and make treaties, as indeed he has made treaties.

Decision-making by one man, no matter how good and fair and just the decisions are, is not proof of national strength or vision, but shameful proof of a people's captivity. No man has the gift of omniscience!

—*Mr. Marcos claims he has launched a revolution to liberate the poor, the dispossessed, the exploited workingmen.* Yet he has banned the workingmen's right to strike and his economic policy deliberately depresses the minimum wage to maintain an attractive atmosphere for foreign as well as local investors. Today, multi-national corporations, the established capitalists, presidential relatives and cronies are shamelessly amassing fortunes while the standard of living of the masses continues to deteriorate day by day.

—Mr. Marcos claims his martial rule is "unique" because it is "compassionate and benevolent." Early this year, Amnesty International released its shocking report on the torture of Filipino political detainees. This report, circulated among the 150 member-nations of the United Nations, denounced the use of "Star Chamber methods on a wide scale to literally torture evidence into existence." The report did not only list the names of the victims but also the names of the torturers. It also detailed and described the various torture techniques employed.

—Mr. Marcos claims he declared martial law to liquidate a subversive movement inspired by Marxist-Leninist-Maoist teachings and beliefs. Yet he is the first Filipino president to "build bridges" to the citadels of communist power—Peking and Moscow—and establish diplomatic relations with practically all the communist states. As if this were not enough, he has publicly acknowledged the "natural leadership of Communist China in the Third World." In a speech delivered in Peking in 1975, Mr. Marcos said:

> I have journeyed today on a mission for the 42 million people of the Republic of the Philippines to assure ourselves that these bridges between our two countries will never be washed *(sic)* again. Because of moral courage that has been manifested and demonstrated by China for all the iniquities of the past and the present, we believe China is the natural leader of the Third World.

—Mr. Marcos declared all-out war against the New People's Army because of its adherence to so-called Mao Tse-tung Thought. But in Peking, in an address before the disciples of the Great Helmsman, Mr. Marcos unabashedly admitted that his New Society was greatly inspired by the "invincible" thoughts and ideas of Chairman Mao:

> I am confident that I shall leave inspired and encouraged in our own modest endeavor in the creation of a New Society for our people, for the transformation of China under the leadership of Chairman Mao Tse-tung is indeed the most noble monument to the invincibility of an idea supported by the force of human spirit.

—Mr. Marcos blamed the oligarchs for most of the ills of the Old Society. Only one member of that oligarchy has been jailed and his family's properties have been appropriated by Mr. Marcos, his family and his cronies. Worse, the so-called New Society has not only coddled the oligarchs of the Old Society, it has spawned new ones—instant millionaires!—who are plundering government financing institutions to finance their corporate raiding and various takeover schemes.

These new oligarchs are being awarded timber, mining and oil concessions and vast tracts of rich government agricultural and urban lands, not to mention lush government construction contracts. Only recently, a presidential crony representing Westinghouse won for its principal the $500 million bid for the construction of the Bataan Nuclear Power Plant in Bagac. His commission was $25 million or P200 million representing five percent of the total bid price. These new oligarchs are greedier, more insatiable and more profligate than the oligarchs of pre-martial law days.

—Mr. Marcos speaks with a bleeding heart for the poor. Yet he has squandered billions of pesos for luxury hotels and convention sites for foreign tourists and international conferences and other non-productive "impact" projects, while barely a few kilometers from these opulent monuments almost a million Filipinos live in filth and squalor, screened from the visitors' view with whitewashed wooden fences, eking out a substandard existence in muddy slums that vividly attest to their grinding poverty.

—Mr. Marcos constantly brags about the "dramatic" improvement of the nation's economy. But he never mentions the massive external debt that his regime has incurred. Eleven years ago, when he first assumed the presidency, the Philippine external debt stood at around $500 million. By September 1972, the external debt was quadrupled to $2.2 billion. Today, the Philippine external debt has passed the $6.4 billion mark and it is still increasing. According to the latest IMF statistics, the Philippines has the highest per capita external debt in Asia. At the rate Mr. Marcos goes on borrowing to finance his projects, the country's foreign debt will in a few more years become one of the biggest in the world.

In September 1972, Congress in one of its last acts approved a P5.3 billion national budget for fiscal year 1972-73. Today, barely five years later, the national budget has passed the P30 billion mark or an increase of about 500 percent over the 1972 level. Only Mr. Marcos really knows how all this money is being squandered and misappropriated.

Daily, our people are being told of the "dramatic" increase in our exports. The records show otherwise. Last year, the Philippines incurred its greatest trade deficit ever—almost $1 billion. This year, economists predict it will be even worse. The "floating peso" has been steadily sinking. The currency market in Hongkong quoted the weak peso at P8.00 to $1, as of November 1, 1977.

Among the five ASEAN countries, the Philippines has the highest interest rates as reported by the *Far Eastern Economic Review* in its November 25, 1977 issue. The Philippines' prime lending rate is 15.5% as compared to Japan's 4.5% and Malaysia's 7.5%. Our inter-bank 24-hour rate is quoted at 14% as against Singapore's 2.5% and Malaysia's and Japan's 4.25%.

Corruption, tagged as one of the major reasons for martial rule, has become more rampant in Mr. Marcos' New Society. Today, greed has run amuck, unchecked by an inquisitive Congress and a vigilant press. The total corruption of this debt-ridden but extravagant Marcos martial law regime is equalled only by its lack of regard for basic human rights.

Last October, 1977, the editors of *Fortune* magazine, after a survey among businessmen operating in the Southeast Asian region, reported that the Philippines "has the second most corrupt government in Southeast Asia"—surpassed only by Indonesia. To do business in the Philippines, you need government connections, the *Fortune* editors reported.

Consider these items from the *Fortune* magazine report on Mr. Marcos' New Society:

1. Without the consent of the people of Manila and environs, Mr. Marcos merged four neighboring cities and thirteen municipalities into a Metro-Manila and again without the consent of the residents of the merged cities and municipalities, he appointed his wife as governor of Metro-Manila—the second most powerful office in the Republic.

Within the boundaries of Metro-Manila live some 20% of the country's population. It is estimated that Metro-Manila easily accounts for at least 70% of gross national receipts. It is the seat of the national government and some 90% of the national government's offices and instrumentalities are located within its environs. Its budget is second only to the national government's.

General Carlos P. Romulo, the Secretary of Foreign Affairs, has described Mrs. Marcos as the *de facto* "Vice President of the Philippines." She is second only to the man who, according to the American columnist William Buckley, is "the executive, the legislature and the judiciary of the Philippines."

In a column that appeared in New York on December 6, 1977, Buckley reported that while Mrs. Marcos is not the *de jure* Vice President of the country by title, she is nevertheless the powerful governor of Metro-Manila. "Not since Robert Moses let New York City slip out his hands has any human being come so close to totally dominate a city," Buckley wrote of Mrs. Marcos. According to Buckley, Mrs. Marcos has merely to look in a particular direction "and before you know it, a huge complex has sprung up."

One of the first acts of the Governor of Metro-Manila was to legalize gambling "to raise revenue" for the new metropolis. A floating casino was allowed to operate exclusively inside the Manila Bay. It is owned and operated by "mysterious" stockholders, according to a major daily. But everyone in Manila knows that behind the floating casino management is the brother of the Metro-Manila Governor. He is today the undisputed gambling czar of the Philippines.

One of the most lucrative gambling establishments in Manila is the Jai-Alai, which was operated by a corporation that received its franchise from the pre-war Commonwealth government. When its franchise expired three years ago, it was not renewed by Mr. Marcos. A new corporation promptly took over management and control of the Jai-Alai fronton. It is now under the management of the new gambling czar, the brother of the First Lady and Metro-Manila Governor.

It is doing a land-office business, because it has been allowed to open off-track betting, an operation denied the former management. The monthly turn-over is in the millions. It is estimated by knowledgeable quarters that the monthly take between the floating casino and the Jai-Alai fronton is more than P2 million a day.

2. Reports of the U.S. Senate and the U.S. Securities and Exchange Commission have described massive million-dollar bribes to officials of the government-backed Philippine Long Distance Telephone Company by the General Telephone and Electric Co. of New York in exchange for supply contracts. PLDT officials should have been investigated for violations of foreign currency regulations and unearned income. None of these U.S. reports has been printed in our kept press. Everything has been hushed up because, as one PLDT official boasted, "an exposé will only hurt the Palace." In the U.S. and Japan, presidents and prime ministers have been driven out of office for similar payolas and wrongdoings.

3. One of the largest corporations in the Philippines before the declaration of martial law was the Manila Electric Co. (MERALCO), owned and controlled by the Lopez family. After martial rule was imposed, it became the prime target for takeover by the Marcos-Romualdez clique. Among the first things "the Clan" did, using the martial law powers as instrument, was: the arrest of the eldest son of Eugenio Lopez, Sr., the major stockholder of MERALCO, for allegedly plotting the assassination of Mr. Marcos.

1973-1974, the Organization of Petroleum Exporting Countries (OPEC) started applying the oil price squeeze. MERALCO, a public utility company that supplies all the power needs of Metro-Manila and environs, was caught in a vicious vise. Its fuel costs started to double, triple, quadruple—but the martial law government's regulatory agency refused to allow them to increase its consumer rates. Within a year, MERALCO teetered on the brink of bankruptcy. Government financing institutions refused to guarantee its foreign loans, with this effect: MERALCO was pushed to the edge of massive defaults in its loans.

It was at this juncture that the Marcos-Romualdez clansmen stepped in. According to the late Eugenio Lopez, Sr., he was promised the release of his eldest son from prison in exchange for the sale of his controlling interest in MERALCO to the Marcos-Romualdez group. After several months of negotiations, faced with massive loan defaults and unchecked OPEC price increases, Mr. Lopez capitulated.

It was sad, the MERALCO grab-squeeze play dealt him. Not only was he forced to "sell", but the terms of the "sale" were never honored—"Never honored," he wept to intimates—by his "buyers". What happened was: Toto Iñing, as Mr. Lopez was called fondly by those who knew him, died without seeing his son, Eugenio Jr., released from the Marcos martial law prison; and he did not live to see the first installment of the MERALCO "sale" price paid by the "purchasers."

After the Marcos-Romualdez takeover, the government regulatory agency *allowed MERALCO to increase its consumer rates*. The government gave covert and overt subsidies. Late this year, the government even agreed to buy all of MERALCO's generating units for a handsome price of over P1 billion. The National Treasury was directed by the Department of Finance to release P700 million in cash to MERALCO in payment for the generating units which Mr. Marcos turned over to the National Power Corporation. The balance of the sale price was to be used to meet MERALCO's outstanding obligations, it was said.

On the fifth anniversary of martial rule, either by malicious design or sheer coincidence, Jesus Bigornia, columnist of *Bulletin Today,* wrote:

> The Manila Electric Company rose to the top of the heap of corporate earners last year. It recorded a stunning P200 million net income or 168% more than that of a year ago. Aside from being authorized to raise electricity rates for household consumers, MERALCO was also exempted from payment of the duty on oil imports, which is some sort of an indirect subsidy *which it should share with the poor consumers.* (Underscoring mine.)

> 4. Late last month, the government moved to take over the other public utility still in private hands. It took over the Philippine Air Lines from Benigno Toda, Jr. When one recalls the Lockheed payola scandals that toppled the Tanaka government in Japan, the Filipino people can only pray that in the announced purchase of Boeing 747 jumbos, PAL will be spared a Lockheed replay, especially now that there is no Congress to look into its internal affairs.

—To dignify his naked power grab, Mr. Marcos describes it as a "Democratic Revolution." It is neither democratic, because in truth and in fact what he has established is a totalitarian regime, nor is it a revolution, because in truth and in fact it is a fascistic executive coup.

One of America's leading students of revolution, Prof. Mark N. Hagopian, in his *The Phenomenon of Revolution,* published in New York in 1974 by Donald Mead and Company, defines a revolution as follows:

> A revolution is an acute, prolonged crisis in one or more of the traditional stratifications (class, status, power) of a political community, which involves a purposive, elite directed attempt to abolish or to reconstruct one or more of said systems by means of an intensification of political power and recourse to violence.

Revolution, in Professor Hagopian's view, differs in scope as well as intensity from other forms of socio-political change and violence. It has a definite, identifiable ideology which infuses a sense of direction and purpose to it that is often lacking in coups, revolts and secessions. Recourse to violence is essential rather than accidental. It is a political phenomenon and its primary goal is the establishment of a new political order—an egalitarian regime, in the case of France; a communist government, in Czarist Russia's case.

If it was not a revolution, then what was it?

Mr. Marcos pulled an executive coup!

According to Professor Hagopian:

> Executive coups vary in form and significance. The most blatant form occurs

when the chief executive of a republic abolishes the existing constitution and pro-
claims himself king or emperor with the intention of founding a dynasty, x x
x (it) *is an unconstitutional and indefinite prolongation of a president's term of
office. (It) occurs when a chief executive tires of opposition stemming from the
legislative branch. In this instance he either disbands, purges, or forcibly coerces
the legislative assembly or replaces it with one that is handpicked.* In some cases,
a veneer of legality is preserved, though usually with the 'suspension' of certain
constitutional guarantees. *(The Phenomenon of Revolution,* p. 7; underscoring
mine)

I do not know whether Professor Hagopian had Mr. Marcos in mind when he
wrote these words.

The good professor warns that an executive coup must not be confused with
"constitutional dictatorship"—or, to borrow Mr. Marcos' favorite expression, "constitutional authoritarianism."

A "constitutional dictatorship," according to Professor Hagopian, "is a *temporary expedient* whereby the executive assumes extraordinary powers *with the
consent of the legislative* in order to deal effectively with grave national emergen-
cies such as war, insurrection, or economic collapse. *In such a case, it is understood
by all that the concentration of powers in the executive will last no longer than
the crisis that necessitated it."* (Underlining supplied, *ibid.*)

—*Finally, Mr. Marcos claims that he has imposed his martial law regime on our
people from the highest and most unselfish motives.* I will concede that he does,
in his own fashion, love our people. The trouble is that, clearly, he does not trust
them. He believes that they will be helpless without him. And I suppose that is
why he keeps them helpless.

Let him be reminded of what the eminent English Catholic author, Chesterton,
has said:

Despotism...and attempts at despotism...are a kind of a disease of the public
spirit. They represent...the drunkenness of responsibility. It is when men begin
to grow desperate in their love for the people, when they are overwhelmed with
the difficulties and blunders of humanity, that they fall back upon a wild desire
to manage everything themselves... The sin and sorrow of despotism is not that
it does not love men, but that it loves them too much and trusts them too little.
Therefore from age to age in history arise these great despotic dreamers...who
have at root this idea, that the world would enter into rest if it went *their* way
and foreswore altogether the right of going on its way. When a man begins to
think that the grass will not grow at night unless he lies awake to watch it, he
generally ends either in an asylum, or on the throne of an emperor.

To go back to our present crisis, what Mr. Marcos has done is essentially the
same as what Hitler did. After installing himself as dictator, Hitler made the peo-

ple of the Saar "vote" away their right to vote. Through rigged referenda, Hitler legitimized his dictatorship. This is what Mr. Marcos has done; he is today the omniscient; the omnipotent!

The plain and simple truth is:

—Mr. Marcos declared martial rule to perpetuate himself in power.

—He deliberately abetted chaos for seven years so that at the end of his constitutionally allowable term he could justify the imposition of martial rule to cover up his mismanagement.

—Having lost his power of persuasion, he has resorted to coercion, to fear— and the complete control of media and other vehicles of mass thought fermentation.

—He established a dictatorship because he knew he had lost the confidence of the people. What he could no longer achieve with the ballot, he grabbed with the bullets of the armed forces.

But let me warn Mr. Marcos of the grave dangers of entrusting the perpetuity of his tenure to the armed forces, as did the Caesars of Rome, his predecessors and preceptors in the practice of martial law. The historian Gibbon tells us:

> Such formidable servants are always necessary but often fatal, to the throne of despotism. By...introducing the Praetorian Guards...into the palace and the Senate, the emperors taught them to perceive their own strength, and the weakness of civil government (and) to view the vices of their masters with familiar contempt...Their pride was nourished by the sense of their irresistible weight; nor was it possible to conceal from them that the person of the sovereign, the authority of the Senate, the public treasure, and the seat of empire, were all in their hands. To divert the Praetorian bands from these dangerous reflections, the firmest and best established princes were obligated to mix blandishments with commands, rewards with punishments; to flatter their pride, indulge their pleasures, connive at their irregularities, and to purchase their precarious faith by a liberal donative.

I now ask Mr. Marcos to reflect on this: Having transformed the armed forces of this Republic into his own private army, having commissioned them to be the instruments of his will rather than the defenders of the commonwealth, and having given them thus a taste of uncontrolled power, for how long will they continue to regard him as their Commander-in-Chief?

Ninoy Aquino's alias, Marcial Bonifacio, as indicated in his passport (inset).
Patiently awaiting his plane at the Los Angeles International Airport (LAX),
August, 1983.

Ninoy as Manila Times correspondent assigned to cover Korea in 1950.

II

THREE GENERATIONS

By our uncompromising resistance we turned him to a terrible tyrant; by his dogged insistence he forced us to become fanatic rebels...

THOMAS JEFFERSON

I AM Benigno S. Aquino, Jr., 45, Filipino, married, father of five, a native of Concepcion, Tarlac, and presently detained since September 23, 1972, at the MSU Compound of the Philippine Army at Fort Bonifacio.

My detention camp is also known as the "cemetery for the living"—to distinguish it from the American Cemetery directly to the north and the Libingan ng mga Bayani (Cemetery of Heroes) slightly to the south.

Both my grandfather and my father were imprisoned, as I now am, for serving the Filipino people.

I am the grandson of the late General Servillano Aquino of the Filipino Revolutionary Army under President Aguinaldo of the First Republic. Shortly after the turn of the century, my grandfather was captured by American forces, tried, convicted and sentenced to death by an American Military Tribunal for "guerilla war crimes even after the capitulation of President Aguinaldo." He escaped execution only after President Theodore Roosevelt declared an amnesty for all Filipino rebels. For six years, my grandfather was imprisoned in the dungeons of Fort Santiago and a grateful nation recognized and rewarded his efforts by naming one of the biggest Philippine Army camps in his honor.

I am the son of the late Benigno S. Aquino, Sr., a former congressman, a senator (majority floor leader), cabinet member under President Quezon during the Philippine Commonwealth, and a Speaker of the National Assembly. He was the No. 2 man of the wartime Second Republic. American authorities imprisoned my father, together with the other members of the wartime government, in Tokyo's Sugamo Prison. He regained his freedom at the birth of the Third Republic in 1946.

I am a product of the Benedictines and of the Jesuit *ratio studiorum*. After twelve years in Catholic educational institutions, I began the study of law at the University of the Philippines.

I am a former newspaperman *(The Manila Times)*. At 17, I was a war correspondent (the Korean War). Later, I became a foreign correspondent (Indo-China, Malaya, Indonesia, the Middle East). In 1955, I was elected mayor of Concepcion, Tarlac. In 1959, I was elected vice governor of Tarlac province. In 1961, I became governor of Tarlac province. I was elected to the same office in 1963. In 1967, I was elected to the Senate of the Philippines.

I was executive assistant to three Presidents: Magsaysay, Garcia, Macapagal. I was awarded decorations by three Presidents: Quirino (The Philippine Legion of Honor, Degree of Officer, for services during the Korean War); Magsaysay (The Philippine Legion of Honor, Degree of Commander, for negotiating the return to the government of Luis M. Taruc, erstwhile Huk Supremo, in 1954); Garcia (First Bronze Anahaw Leaf to the PLH-Officer, for services in the peace and order campaign; Presidential Merit Award for intelligence work in Indonesia, in 1958, "classified"). In awarding me the highest civilian award of the Republic, President Magsaysay cited my "invaluable contribution to the collapse of the communist-led Huk insurgency."

I am not a communist. I have never been one. I have never joined any communist party. I am not—and have never been—a member of any illegal and/or subversive organization, or even a front organization.

Yes, I have met with communist leaders and members of subversive organizations both as a newspaperman and as a public servant as far back as 1954. In fact, the government awarded me the highest civilian award precisely for what my pacification parleys with rebels and subversives had achieved.

President Magsaysay made use of my services as a negotiator not only with the communist-led dissidents in Central Luzon but also with Muslim outlaw leaders. Indeed, I consider my ability to communicate with the leaders of the various dissident movements as well as my understanding of their causes as one of my special qualifications for high office.

I have been a student of communism, especially the Philippine communist movement, for the last two decades. I have written many papers, delivered many lectures on the Huks, who later became the HMBs and who, still later, became the CPP/NPAs, their aims, their inner dynamics and motivations, both in the Philippines and abroad.

If I had planned to seek the Presidency in 1973, it was because I sincerely believed I had the key to the possible final solution to the vexing dissident (communist) problem.

I was first exposed to communism as a young teenager shortly after the war, in 1945, when my hometown of Concepcion was literally occupied by the Hukbalahaps. Our town mayor, an avowed Huk, was appointed by the dissident group.

In 1950, I was assigned by the *Manila Times* to cover the UN police action in Korea with special emphasis on the participation of the Philippine Expeditionary Force to Korea (PEFTOK). I witnessed the brutal massacre of innocent civilians by fleeing communist forces. Barely 18, I learned first-hand from North Korean survivors how the communists governed and regimented their people, how all their freedoms were suppressed, especially the rights to peaceful assembly, religion and free speech. Some of my most poignant early newspaper stories dwelt on the grimness of existence under communist totalitarian rule.

At 20, I was assigned as a foreign correspondent in Indo-China. I was at Dien Bien Phu and covered the last dying moments of French colonialism in Asia. Later, I was posted to Malaya to cover the British counter-insurgency efforts under General Templar. In 1954, I returned to the Philippines and negotiated Mr. Taruc's return to the government fold on May 16, 1954.

Three former Presidents availed of my services, especially in the field of counter-insurgency. I was special assistant to President Magsaysay when I met Taruc. Under President Garcia, I was entrusted with the delicate mission of monitoring the so-called "Colonels' Revolt" in Indonesia. Under President Macapagal, I served as his special assistant in his travels to Cambodia and Indonesia at the height of the Malaysia-Indonesia *konfrontasi*.

In 1965, President Macapagal appointed me spokesman of the Philippine Delegation to the crucial Afro-Asian conference in Algiers where the two Communist super-powers, the USSR and the PRC, girded for a showdown. The Philippine Delegation, together with a handful of "free world" delegations, held the balance of power. Fortunately, or unfortunately, a bomb was exploded inside the conference hall on the eve of the meeting, forcing the organizers to "indefinitely postpone the conference."

In 1970, I was a member of the Philippine delegation to the Djakarta Conference on Cambodia which took up the entry of American and South Vietnamese forces into that country.

In fact, four days before the martial law declaration, Senator Gerardo Roxas and I were given a highly classified briefing by the AFP general staff on the nation's counter-insurgency plans at Camp Aguinaldo.

I enjoyed the highest security clearance from the government.

I have been a student of theoretical Marxism. I have followed every twist and turn of our local communists. I have read practically all the published works of our local Reds. Whenever possible, I interviewed communist intellectuals to get first-hand information.

This, however, does not mean that I have embraced communism, much less joined any communist or subversive organization. On the contrary, I would like to believe that I convinced some of the dissidents to return to the fold of the government, as in the case of Mr. Taruc.

I have never advocated the overthrow of the government by force and violence, much less the establishment of a totalitarian regime. Or worse, placing this country under the domination and control of an alien power.

I have no reason to do that—not I, of all people. Why should I advocate a violent overthrow of our government? I am one of the lucky few who never lost an election—from mayor, to vice governor, to governor, to senator. Why should I want to destroy a form of government that has served me well? In fact, in 1972, I was within a stone's throw from the highest office within the gift of our people— the Presidency.

It is true I urged our people to boot Mr. Marcos out of office. I campaigned vigorously against him in 1965 and again in 1969. I warned our people as early as 1968 of Mr. Marcos' sinister plot to suspend our elections and perpetuate himself in power through the declaration of martial rule. I denounced in my maiden privilege speech in the Senate Mr. Marcos' gradual and steady development of a "Garrison State." For four years before September, 1972, I warned our people of Mr. Marcos' creeping militarism.

Mr. Marcos is not the Republic and the State. It is unfortunate that some people hold the belief that to oppose Mr. Marcos is to oppose the State and that opposition to Marcos is tantamount to treason.

I am against Mr. Marcos. But I am a loyal citizen of the Republic!

III

PHILIPPINE COMMUNISM

**Political power grows out of
the barrel of a gun.**

—MAO TSE-TUNG

The great attraction of Marxism is its so-called "historical inevitability." Marx held: Evolution of human society, as the human race has known it, is inexorable; the Third Estate, the bourgeois class, will go the way of the liquidated nobles and clergy in the "next revolutionary act," which will pave the way for the dictatorship of the proletariat and create the classless or socialist society, at which point the class struggles shall cease and come to a final rest, because it shall be a harmonious and unanimous society—the perfect society.

It will surely happen, because it must happen. Such are the inexorable laws of history, according to Marx.

From these "inexorable" premises, Marx posited that social classes were determined by their relationship to the means of production. Feudal society, with its lords and vassals, had been succeeded in Western Europe by bourgeois society with its capitalists and workers; but bourgeois society contained within itself the seeds of its own destruction: the number of capitalists would diminish, while the ranks of the impoverished proletariat would grow until there would be a breakdown to be followed by a socialist revolution in which the overwhelming majority, the proletariat, would dispossess the small minority of capitalist exploiters.

The modern state, according to Marx, was "nothing more than a committee for the administration of the consolidated affairs of the bourgeois class as a whole"; the rulers of this state bore the "total guilt" for all the exploitations and deprivations, sufferings and grievances, of the workingmen; to remove them was to cure all evil, to overthrow them would be worth every sacrifice and justified any means. Then he pointed the way: the rulers were so few, so isolated; they were not invincible; they could be attacked, must be attacked.

It was, for Marx, the remedy to end poverty, to end class war, to end international war—and to create a new civilization in which exploitation, acquisitiveness and social antagonisms would not exist, and which would usher in an era of peace and abundance for all men.

For the working class, it was a siren song. As Marx put it, the choice was: between absolute property maintained by the force of the few and absolute property abolished by the dictatorship of the proletariat.

Marx based his theoretical framework on his so-called laws of dialectics:

1. Quantitative changes produce qualitative changes and vice versa;
2. Negation of negations: one thing grows out of another, then does battle with it. The newly grown produces in itself the seed of its own destruction; and
3. The interpenetration of opposites: that there are objective contradictions and resolutions in the world.

Many writers have already written voluminous dissertations on these so-called laws. C. Wright Mills, for example, believes that these "mysterious laws of dialectics" merely afford self-appointed insiders an "intellectually-cheap way into mysterious insights, a substitute for the hard work of learning." To believe in the fulfillment of the Marxian promise, the dictatorship of the proletariat, Walter Lippmann argued with persuasive historical evidence, is to be touched with naivete; what communists deliver, instead, is "a dictatorship over the proletariat."

I will limit my discussion to the catalogue of ideas that I gathered in my many conversations with local communist intellectuals as they related theoretical Marxism and Lenin's interpretations to the Philippine situation. To sum up their views:

1. The economic basis of a society determines its socio-political structure as a whole, as well as the psychology of the people within it. The Philippines has a capitalist economy. In all class societies, the state is the coercive instrument of the owning and, therefore, governing class—the capitalists.

2. The functional indispensability of a class in the economic system leads to its political supremacy. In the Philippines, for example, to be successful in politics, one has to have money. Money can come only from the capitalists. Hence, the governors are in fact beholden to those who control the purse strings. The entire machinery of government inevitably draws its direction and guidance from the

primary source of power which is money, which is the capitalist—the true puppeteer.

3. There is no such thing as true public opinion in a capitalist system. The press and other media are owned and controlled by a handful of wealthy families. Every day, through the media, the working class is brainwashed to accept its exploitation.

4. The class struggle between owners and workers is the social, political and psychological reflection of objective economic conflicts. Class struggle, rather than harmony, natural or otherwise, is the moral and inevitable condition in a capitalist society.

5. In a capitalist society, the workers cannot escape their exploited condition. No matter what they do, they will receive only token reforms. Only by armed revolution will they find true liberation from exploitation, "because exploitation is built into capitalism as an economic system."

6. The dynamic of historical change is the conflict between the forces of production and the relations of production. The rich get richer; the poor, poorer. This will lead inevitably to an explosion. It is inexorable: the small exploiting capitalist minority must give way to the forces of change in the same way the feudal barons gave way to the bourgeoisie.

7. History is on the side of the communist. Capitalism is involved in one economic crisis after another. These crises are getting worse. So capitalism moves into its final crisis, the revolution of the proletariat. Only by destroying the capitalist system can the workingmen free themselves from exploitation. Although men make their own history, given the circumstances of the economic foundation, the way they make it and the direction it takes are determined. The course of history is structurally limited to the point of being inexorable.

8. The post-capitalist society will first pass through a transitional state, that of the dictatorship of the proletariat. Then it will move into a higher phase in which true communism will prevail. The state will eventually wither away, for the only function of the state is to hold down the exploited class.

From these theoretical Marxist postulates, local communist intellectuals moved on to adopt Lenin's interpretations as expressed in Lenin's voluminous writings.

Lenin, one of the first to put into practice what Marx theorized, envisioned a three-stage scenario for a communist takeover. In his seminal work, *What Is To Be Done,* published in 1902, Lenin wrote:

> First: at the start, workers have no revolutionary consciousness, having been brainwashed by the capitalist media. Their spontaneous actions will only lead to 'trade union' demands and not to revolution; Second: revolutionary consciousness must be brought to the workers from the outside by their intellectual

leaders; and Third: there must be a party of full-time, disciplined, centrally directed professionals capable of acting as one man who will form the vanguard of the proletarian revolution. These professionals will belong to a party, the Communist Party. The Communist Party will exercise the dictatorship of the proletariat during the transitional period.

Guided by classical Marxism as interpreted by Lenin, local communist leaders have adopted the following program of action:

1. Establish the Communist Party of the Philippines as the historical agency of the revolution. These leaders hold that a socialist revolution can occur in a backward country even in the early stages of capitalist development. But the party must be tightly organized, disciplined and composed of professional revolutionaries who will conduct both legal and/or illegal action to awaken and eventually represent the proletariat.

2. The end, which is the accomplishment of the revolution, justifies the means even if it calls for a violent overthrow of the government, liquidation of opponents and counter-revolutionaries, etc. The armed forces of the state must be harassed and eventually defeated in a final combat. It is imperative, therefore, that a military arm for the party must be organized—the New People's Army. Politically and morally, violence and conspiracy are part and parcel of the revolution and are fully justified. Morality means doing what has to be done to make a revolution, provided you accept morally its historical consequences.

3. The capitalist world has entered its imperialist phase, an age of great financial networks of monopoly capital. But the capitalists are at each other's throats over the spoils of exploitation. Capitalism is now in its death throes.

4. Imperialism has produced war as the capitalists outdid themselves in despoiling and exploiting the undeveloped world. The exploited people are awakening to the evils of imperialism. Under the leadership of professional revolutionaries, the enlightened workers will take the decisive step toward a genuine proletarian revolution.

5. The CPP/NPA, the historical agency by which the revolution is firmly led, if not made, must maintain its structure as a revolutionary organization after it has won the power of the state. "It will be the only party because it is the only true representative of the workers and the peasants." It cannot tolerate divisive dissent. Any public disagreement after a party decision has been reached by the controlling group amounts to treason.

6. The old state, the old capitalist society, must be completely destroyed and a new state machinery must be set up by the Communist Party. There will be only one party, because the key to success is political monopoly.

This dogma of the dominant single party as enunciated by Lenin has been adopted by the CPP/NPA which even prohibits factions within the party. Very clearly, in a Philippines dominated by the CPP/NPA, there is no room for the Liberals, the Nacionalistas or even the Socialist Party of the Philippines.

There will be no need for us politicians.

IV

THE FILIPINO AS DISSIDENT

He is ready to accept punishments for his
behavior, ready to pay the price of his
convictions. His violation of the law is
undertaken in behalf of a higher principle.
He hopes to stir the conscience of society...
We are all Vietcong.

—JERRY RUBIN

The last temptation is the greatest treason:
To do the wrong deed for the right reason.

—T.S. ELIOT

I N 1954, when I first established contact with Huk Supremo Luis M. Taruc, high government policymakers held as dogmatic truth that our insurgents were communist-led, if not all communists.

After my series of interviews with Taruc, I reported to President Magsaysay my basic findings: that the Huks led by Taruc were primarily agrarian reformers with valid grievances against landowners and government forces; that they were smarting from American discrimination in the recognition of guerrilla rights; that they were more socialists than communists. This report stirred a controversy. The President's military advisers to a man denounced my report as "naive and totally erroneous."

In my interviews with him, Taruc emphasized time and again that he was a socialist, a follower of the late Pedro Abad Santos, the founder of the Socialist Party of the Philippines. And as early as our first contact, I was deeply impressed by Mr. Taruc's religious faith.

In all my dialogues with dissident field commanders in Luzon, I never met one who really understood the basic theories of Marx and/or Lenin, or its latest variant, the so-called Mao Tse-tung Thought. Most of them admitted having undergone some schooling in the underground "Stalin universities" during the fifties and the sixties where Philippine revolutionary history and basic communist theories were the major fare. But few really went beyond mouthing the shopworn formulas, the cliche's regarding the evils of "imperialism, feudalism and bureaucrat capitalism."

This does not mean that there are no capable communist intellectuals in our country. There are, but they have not succeeded in truly educating their mass base beyond the routine slogans and catch-phrases.

The basic cry has remained the same: Land for the landless! And a litany of real and imagined grievances against landowners, the government, the military and the local police agencies, who in the Huk's view invariably sided with the rich in any conflict with the poor.

The Magsaysay approach to the dissident problem was effective, because he instinctively understood the basic motivations of the insurgent. He offered land to the landless. And he committed his administration to this principle, which he himself enunciated: "Those who have less in life, should have more in law."

When offered the opportunity to own land of their own, Huk rank and filers surrendered by the hundreds. Many were resettled in EDCOR farms hacked out of the jungles by army engineers. These are now bustling communities.

In 1956, shortly after my election as mayor of Concepcion, Tarlac, one of my first efforts was to contact the Huk leaders operating in my jurisdiction. I went to them unarmed, unescorted.

With the consent of President Magsaysay, I told them my plans for our town and outlined my policies. I promised them free movement within my jurisdiction, freedom to proselytize and win the barrio people to their cause peacefully. I even named a barrio contact man for every barrio whom they could go to should they have any complaints or message for me. The only condition I imposed was: No killing.

PC records will bear me out. During my twelve years as mayor of Concepcion, vice governor and governor of Tarlac, Huk/HMB killings were at their lowest levels. After I left office in 1967, HMB-NPA killings increased by more than 500%—an average of 100 killings yearly, from 1968 to 1972.

Huk Supremo Luis Taruc discussing surrender terms with Ninoy, President Ramon Magsaysay's emissary in 1954.

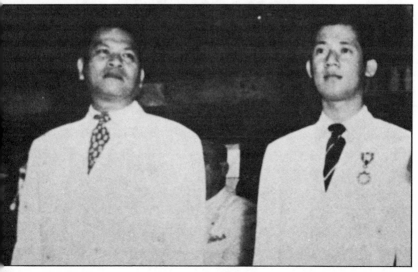

Ninoy, with President Ramon Magsaysay, after receiving the Legion of Honor Award in 1954.

Ninoy-Cory wedding with President Ramon Magsaysay as sponsor.

Presidents Magsaysay, Garcia and Macapagal knew of my policy of "coexistence." I briefed every incoming 1st PC Zone commander and his staff. I told them of my willingness to engage the dissidents in open political combat. I was confident that, in any open election, our people would opt for our system of government so long as the government officials were faithful to their trust. I never lost a single political contest in Tarlac. In fact, I broke my own electoral records.

As late as 1969, the revitalized CPP/NPA fought us head-on politically. Again PC records will show that in 1969, there were three congressional candidates for Tarlac's second district: Atty. Tomas Matic, for the NP; Rep. Jose V. Yap, the incumbent, for the LP; and Atty. Max Llorente, for the CPP/NPA group. It is true Atty. Max Llorente gave our LP candidate a stiff fight in the towns of Capas, Bamban and Concepcion, where the CPP/NPA cadres were strongest. But in the final tally, he trailed miserably behind our LP candidate.

Once again, we proved the validity of our policy. In an open political combat, the communists could not win popular support.

But the rebels have their usefulness to some barrio residents. Some HMB/NPA bands waged unrelenting war against cattle rustlers in areas where local police forces were lax, were unresponsive or, worse, were in connivance with the criminals.

In several land and tenancy disputes, HMB/NPA commanders invariably sided with the poor exploited farmers and brought pressure on the land-owners. In some extreme cases, landowners were liquidated, especially if they proved unrepentant and recalcitrant. Rebel justice was often swift and without cost to the litigants, thus winning the respect, if not the silent support, of the unlettered peasant.

It is almost axiomatic that where the government is weak and unresponsive, the rebels are invariably strong and popular. In situations like this, the rebels are indeed the people's army.

To this day, I still believe the mass of our dissidents can be persuaded to return to the fold if the government adopts a liberal policy of attraction and resettlement; if the government adopts a liberal policy of attraction and resettlement; if the government pursues a genuine, progressive land reform program that will not only give land to the tillers but assistance to the farmers to free them from the clutches of usurers; if petty corruption at the lowest level is curbed; and if the government can bring modern technology to the farmer and provide him some protection from the vagaries of nature.

In 1961, under the sponsorship of NEC-US AID, I launched Operation Spread (Systematic Program for Rural Economic Assistance and Development) in Tarlac. In less than two years, rice yields increased by 30%. New grains, like sorghum and hybrid corn, were introduced to augment the feed grains for our infant livestock industry.

In the Senate, I tried to acquaint my colleagues with the dynamics and motivations of the insurgency movement in Central Luzon to give them a better perspective of the problem. I assisted Senator Salvador H. Laurel's Committee on Justice in its in-depth study of the dissident problem. Its report has since become a major resource paper on Philippine insurgency.

In my speeches, both in and out of Congress, I advocated a more humane approach to the dissident problem. I denounced the use of para-military units, like the Monkees, who summarily executed barrio residents suspected of NPA links. My exposes brought me into a collision course with Mr. Marcos and his military subordinates.

In May 1966, barely five months in office, Mr. Marcos branded me a "Huk coddler and sympathizer" when I, as governor of Tarlac, denounced the massacre of farmers in Barrio Culatingan, Concepcion, Tarlac, by a group of Monkees led by a PC Ranger. It is indeed an ironical twist that while I stand today charged with communist subversion, Mr. Marcos is adopting some of my recommendations in 1966: a liberal program of amnesty for returning dissidents, resettlement and a vigorous land reform program.

In 1969-1970, I joined a majority Senate group that wanted Republic Act No. 1700, the "Anti-Subversion Act," repealed because it had not only outlived its usefulness, it was a major stumbling block to the normalization of diplomatic relations with the socialist countries, including the two communist super-powers.

During the Senate Committee on Finance deliberations on the budget, I consistently batted for increased capital expenditures and appropriations for social services while limiting the Armed Forces outlay to no more than 10% of the total national budget. We, the Liberals, never succeeded in our efforts to keep the AFP budget below the 10% target. Year after year, we were voted down by the sheer numbers of Mr. Marcos' Nacionalistas, after months of debates and filibusters.

Before civic audiences, I warned our people that time was running out—that if we Filipinos did not reform our society peacefully, we would be reformed violently by a communist-led upheaval.

In various speeches and writings, I urged the abolition of special privileges. I denounced government corruption in many Senate speeches, and my exposes sparked numerous Senate Blue Ribbon investigations.

Many of our countrymen have been conditioned to automatically believe that the dissidents, be they Huks, HMBs or CPP/NPAs, are not only communists or communist-led, but are evil personified. I do not believe they are *per se evil*. Assuming they are evil, they are a necessary evil.

Were it not for the Huks, President Magsaysay would never have pushed through Congress the landmark Rice Tenancy Act, which provided for tenants' security of tenure and the itemization of the division of produce. Known as the 70-30 Rice Law, that law for the first time gave the tenant the sole option to remain a tenant or become a lessee.

All our Presidents have pursued social reform programs in reaction to dissident unrest. Let us go down the list:

President Quezon proclaimed his "social justice" program as a direct result of the unrest spawned by the *Anak Pawis*, the *Colorums*, the *Sakdalistas* and other rebel groups during the twenties and the thirties.

Presidents Roxas and Quirino had ambivalent Huk policies. But they nevertheless pursued a liberal policy towards labor—and they expropriated the so-called friar lands and other feudal estates for re-distribution to their tenants.

President Garcia pushed for more liberal labor laws in addition to his Filipino First policy.

And when Macapagal, a son of Central Luzon, was elected President, the country witnessed the enactment of the first comprehensive Land Reform Code in the Philippines, seminal though it was. Congress passed it in 1963; but only after President Macapagal had called the reluctant Congress to several special sessions, wearying the landed interests in the Senate and the House until they gave in. This is the Land Reform Code now being implemented by Mr. Marcos.

Indeed, our wealthy Filipinos have yielded only under mounting social pressure—never of their own volition. Without the Sakdals, without the Huks, without the NPAs, our toiling people would still be serfs in a *kasama* or land tenancy system as feudal as in any feudal state.

The dissidents, I concede, have committed many acts of murder and depredation. Many have already paid for their crimes with their lives or with long prison terms. But it must be equally admitted that because of their unremitting struggle, our society and our people's social conditions have improved.

When the muse of history writes the Filipino saga, free of bias and prejudice, I am sure the Filipino dissident will be given his rightful share of praise and gratitude in the struggle to free and improve the lot of the Filipino poor.

I have seen young rebels die in combat. Outnumbered, they stood their ground and went bravely to their death.

I have seen many of them wearing tattered clothes, hunted like wild animals in the mountains of Tarlac, sleeping on bare earth inside sugar cane plantations with nothing more than a small plastic sheet to shelter them from the elements, going without food for days. These young men endured all hardships without complaining.

They should have been in schools studying. Yet, without compensation, they left their homes and loved ones and engaged in a lonely struggle against over-whelming odds.

Many of these young rebels died unlamented and unsung!

Yes, there were times I marvelled at their simple idealism and unalloyed courage. In their own fashion, they were patriots!

But let us not forget: This Republic was founded by rebels and insurgents who were hunted down like mad dogs in their own time. My own grandfather was one of those hunted men. Some of our greatest heroes—Frs. Gomez, Burgos and Zamora; Jose Rizal and Andres Bonifacio—were all executed for treason. Yesterday's traitors are today's heroes!

Who knows but that fifty years from now, a province, a huge military camp, a major national highway, will be named after young rebels who today are branded as traitors and shot on some God-forsaken mountain.

If I have gone out of my way to meet with insurgents, if I have given them shelter and medical aid when they came to me, bleeding and near death, it was because I was convinced these dissidents were freedom-fighters first—in their own light—and if they were communists at all, they were communist last.

One of the most moving parables of Jesus Christ is the story of the Good Samaritan who helped the injured Jew, the sworn enemy of his sect. Abandoned and ignored by his fellow Jews, the wounded man was saved by his own enemy. Jesus Christ gave mankind only one commandment: Love. Love your God and your neighbor. And to Jesus, even your worst enemy is your neighbor.

I never wanted even our worst rebels to feel isolated from government. I wanted to give them the opportunity to air their grievances to a nationally elected Senator of the Republic who would make their voices and their demands heard in the Senate.

They might have been dissidents. But to me they were brother Filipinos who deserved the right to be heard. My intention was to prevent them from becoming hopelessly desperate—and to give them a feeling of belonging. By lending them a hand and a sympathetic ear, I wanted to hold out to them the hope for a better future.

If this is treason, if this is subversion, I am ready to be punished.

V

A CHRISTIAN DEMOCRATIC VISION

> Teacher, which is the greatest command-
> ment in the Law?...Love God...Love your
> neighbor as yourself.
>
> —MATT. 22: 34-26
> MARK 12: 28-37;
> LUKE 20: 41-44
>
> You cannot make a revolution if you
> don't have the courage to hurt your own
> bourgeoisie.
>
> —SEMBENE OUSMANE

A S I DELVED deeper into the underlying reasons behind our chronic insurgency problem, I came to a realization: The accepted notions of our
capitalist system must be thoroughly reviewed, some very basic capitalist
doctrines must be totally discarded.

I also concluded: The answer does not lie in the extreme solution of communism.

In time, I came to accept: Capitalism must be reformed by an ideology that
will restore the original balance between economic and political freedom.

Capitalism must be corrected by vigorous anti-monopoly legislation, sup-
plemented more positively by social welfare and security measures than now ex-

ist. Basic economic decisions must be made by the community—the government—and not by the private owners of the means of production. More efficient national economic planning must be adopted to husband our meager resources and bring the greatest good to the greatest number.

Individual economic independence must be restored under conditions set by the people themselves.

It was this realization that prompted me to call for the nationalization of our basic and strategic industries during the late sixties. I proposed then that all public utilities—for a start—should come under government ownership. In the area of mass transit, for example, I advocated a measure of subsidy to alleviate the difficulties of the working poor. In the Senate, I joined the sponsors of land reform and urban housing development for the masses.

One of the reasons I joined the Liberal Party in 1963 was because I was convinced by President Macapagal's welfare state program. I saw it as a step, humble though it was, towards the removal of the great social and economic imbalances in our country—the main causes of our continuing unrest.

If I must be labeled, I think I will fit the label of Christian Socialist best. My ideology flows from the mainstream of Christian Democratic Socialism as practiced in Austria, West Germany and the Scandinavian countries.

I believe that in a democracy, political power is a sacred trust that must be held for the benefit of the people.

I believe that freedom of the individual is all-important and ranks above everything else. Every citizen must be given the equal opportunity to self-fulfillment, to better himself. While it is true indeed that not all men are equally endowed, I believe that every man should be given the equal opportunity for advancement through free, universal and quality education.

Confidence between the majority and the minority, between the government and the governed, is indispensable to the vitality of a democracy. There can be no confidence where established rights are destroyed by fiat.

The supreme value of democracy is freedom, not property. The democratic world will meet the communist challenge if it upholds and unites on the issue of freedom as the fundamental element of human survival.

I believe that once the life of freedom is guaranteed, the question of economic institutions, of private or public enterprise, will take care of itself.

A free media is indispensable if a democracy is to function efficiently, if it is to be real. The people, who are sovereign, must be adequately informed all the time. A reasonable case, reasonably presented, will eventually win the hearts of the people. But the people must know the facts if one expects them to decide correctly.

I believe democracy is not just majority rule, but informed majority rule, and with due respect for the rights of minorities. It means that while the preference of the majority must prevail, there should be full opportunity for all points of view to find expression. It means toleration for opposition opinions. Where you find suppression of minority opinion, there is no real democracy.

The basic flaw of capitalism is its primary concern for political liberty; it cares comparatively less about social and economic equality. Communism, on the other hand, aims at social and economic equality but ruthlessly opposes and destroys political liberty.

I believe in a Christian Democratic Socialist ideology that will harmonize political freedom with social and economic equality, taking and merging the best of the primary conflicting systems—communism and capitalism.

I have said, and say it here again: I am not a communist, never was, and never will be! These are my reasons:

1. Communism calls for violence in the overthrow of existing institutions regardless of the cost in human lives. The individual's interest is subordinated to that of the state. It aims to establish a dictatorship under a one-party system. *It tolerates no truth other than itself!*

As Engels bluntly put it, in a letter to Bebel:

> As the State is only a transitional institution which we are obliged to use in the revolutionary struggle, in order to crush our enemies by force, it is pure nonsense to speak of a free people's State. During the period that the proletariat *needs* the State, it needs it, not in the interests of freedom, but in the interest of crushing its antagonists; and when it becomes possible really to speak of freedom, the State as such will cease to exist. (Quoted in Lenin's *State and Revolution*, pp. 170-171, Vanguard Press, 1926)

And as Lenin himself wrote:

> Dictatorship is an authority relying directly upon force, and not bound by any laws. The revolutionary dictatorship of the proletariat is an authority maintained by means of force over and against the bourgeoisie, and not bound by any law. (Lenin, *The Proletarian Revolution*, p. 15)

I believe in evolutionary reform and I regard all human life as equally priceless, regardless of circumstances. I hold individual freedom most sacred, because it is God's gift. I cannot accept any form of dictatorship, whether of the left, the right or the center.

2. Revolutionary communism visualizes the transition from capitalist enterprise

to public ownership as a sudden, violent and complete act. There is no payment or compensation for expropriated property, because it considers capitalist property, morally and socially, as little better than theft. It is committed dogmatically to the principle of public ownership of all forms of property, excepting only personal consumer goods.

3. I am not committed to any *a priori* dogma of the inherent supremacy of public ownership over private. I believe in the Christian Socialist ideology that seeks to establish a set of rational, pragmatic, empirically verifiable criteria that qualify an industry for nationalization. I agree that monopolies in private hands must never be allowed. I also believe that basic and strategic industries must be nationalized, because it is too dangerous to leave the determination of national needs and priorities in the hands of a few. My primary concern is national interest and the general welfare, not nationalization.

I am for the payment of just compensation for the expropriation of property, but I hold that the state should regulate the re-investment of these compensatory funds. For example, funds paid landowners in the expropriation sale of their ricelands should not be allowed to be invested in overseas or foreign ventures, or even in any of the nation's other regions. The government should set up industries where the expropriated lands are located, then exchange stocks in these industries for the land bonds paid the landowners.

In this way, two things are accomplished: There is no capital flight from the region and additional job opportunities for non-farm workers are created. If capital flight is allowed, landowners will reinvest their funds in, say, Manila; during the amortization period, there will be a steady capital drain from the original region.

I adhere to an evolutionary program. This must always stand the test of national approval as expressed through periodic elections, plebiscites, referenda, which will ensure that the program is implemented—and will continue to be implemented—only with the consent of the majority freely expressed.

4. In communism, the opposition is liquidated. I believe the opposition must be won over.

Lenin held that workers under capitalism are mentally enslaved to the capitalist ideology and incapable of peaceful conversion to socialism without changing first the economic structure of society. Violence, he said, is the sole vehicle for change because the capitalist will yield only to force. To use a much-abused cliche, "Political power grows out of the barrel of a gun."

Lenin based his justification of Communist Party rule on the assumption that the masses are incapable of understanding and acting "correctly." They must be led, Lenin held, by "a dedicated band of selfless revolutionary professionals" who possess the "correct knowledge of the laws of history and society." He advocated not a dictatorship *of* but *over* the proletariat! In this, his apologia for authoritarianism did not differ from any other apology for tyranny.

Finally, Lenin argued that because communists are engaged in a ceaseless strug-gle, a class war which is always a ruthless conflict, the communist has no room for sentimentality, for romanticism, but must use all possible tactical and strategic means, whether legal or illegal, to reach his objectives. This is, shorn of Leninist jargon: the revolutionary seizure of power. It is, said Lenin, the only way.

I am a humanist, a democrat and a romantic. And this is where I part company with the communists.

In 1969, I visited the Soviet Union on the invitation of the USSR Friendship Society. I was allowed to bring a television crew to film my tour and interviews. I saw the great progress made by that mighty communist regime. In less than six-ty years, Russia had emerged from backwardness to the status of a super-power!

The people looked well-fed. Everyone seemed to be employed. The universities were full of eager students. Cost of living was kept at a stable minimum. From all appearances indeed, communist Russia was the dreamed-of Utopia where unemployment, hunger and want had been banished.

But I left Russia with a distinct feeling—that there was something lacking in the Soviet paradise. On reflection, I realized what was lacking: there was a lack of color and variety; miles and miles of high-rise apartments which all looked the same; the people rarely smiled.

In the exhibition parks where the Sputniks and the latest Soviet farm equipment were displayed, there were thousands of ogling Russians but very few talked to a foreigner. I got the impression from my interviews with people that they weigh-ed every word they spoke. They were uneasy speaking to a foreigner.

Yes, the Russian people had their bread. But they had lost their freedom!

According to Aleksandr Solzhenitsyn, the Russians still crave for freedom, but they have lost the will to fight for it:

> x x x we are waiting for freedom to fall on our lap like some unexpected miracle, without any effort on our part, while we ourselves do nothing to win it. Never mind the old traditions of supporting people in political trouble, feeding the fugitive, sheltering the passless and the homeless (we might lose our state-controlled jobs). We labor day by day, conscientiously and sometimes even with talent, to strengthen our common prison.

Solzhenitsyn said that if the Russian people had only willed to live on a crust of bread and be honest, they would be free and invincible.

On the eve of his exile, he gave this parting judgment of his people which may well be a universal diagnosis:

"We have got what we deserved!"

VI

MANIFESTO FOR A FREE SOCIETY

> To us, both freedom and equality are
> precious and essential to human hap-
> piness. They are the twin pillars upon
> which the ideal of human brotherhood
> rests...the ultimate aim of political
> activity is the fullest development
> of every human personality.
>
> —1962 OSLO DECLARATION
> OF THE SOCIALIST
> INTERNATIONAL

IN THE MOST unequivocal terms, not a few communist leaders have told me that there is no room for politicians in the CPP/NPA set-up. To them, all politicians are a product of the "comprador, bourgeois-capitalist system" which must be eliminated.

I have discussed my "ideology" with them. And the biggest surprise of my life: They not only rejected it but held it as more dangerous than the outright capitalist ideology.

I tried to explain to them that the Filipino is not one who is comfortable in an extreme position, that the Filipino is basically a peaceful, spiritual, if not a religious man. I was, they told me to my face, "historically wrong." I believe not. And the freedom that is born of the spirit remains the foundation of my ideology, my life's credo.

I think I can best explain my ideology by excerpting from a manifesto I wrote last year after my 40-day hunger strike to protest the judicial (dis) processes under the present martial rule. On the advice of my Jesuit spiritual adviser, I wrote down the outlines of my ideal society. Part of my Manifesto reads as follows:

"WE DREAM

OF A COMMUNITY OF LIBERATED CITIZENS enjoying the full benefits of a Free Society:

—FREE to choose, criticize and remove our duly elected governors;

—FREE from the imprisoning walls of ignorance, poverty and disease;

—FREE from the exploitation of a privileged and propertied few; and

—FREE from the entangling webs of super-power hegemony, imperialism and neo-colonialism.

"WE BELIEVE

WE ARE THE PEOPLE OF GOD

ENDOWED with reason—which lifts us from the brute—from which we derive our standards of morality, justice and the rational method of ascertaining our duty to our fellowmen and our community.

ENDOWED with a free will and slave to no one, save our Maker. Exercising our free will, we enter into an agreement with all citizens on basic and fundamental tenets, to which we all adhere—and which we pledge to protect—to further the commonweal and our communal interests.

A FREE SOCIETY reconciles liberty and equality; rejects liberal freedom without equality and total equality without freedom. Its essence is the absence of special privilege. Its guarantee is an equal opportunity for self-fulfillment for every citizen. It is dynamic, not static, open to change, be it gradual or rapid, for no one does possess the last word, and the world of men and nature is in constant flux.

LABOR is the most effective human principle; social interest the fundamental stimulus to economic activity. Ultimately, all basic and strategic means of production must come under social ownership to ensure equitable proration of the national wealth and to safeguard the national interest.

THE DIALECTIC OF POWER AND RESISTANCE is one of the great motive forces of history. Power produces conflict and conflict between antagonistic forces gives rise to ever new solutions.

AN OPPOSITION PARTY is indispensable in a democracy. The opposition should act as the critic of the party in power, developing, defining, and presenting the policy alternatives which are necessary for a true

Ninoy with a Muslim leader.

Ninoy being entertained by a number of Muslim leaders and officials.

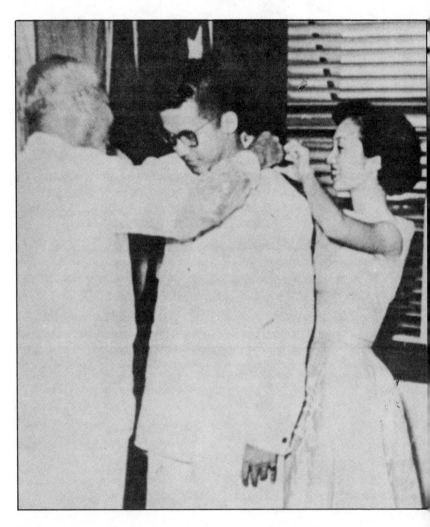

Cory assisting Defense Secretary Sotero Cabahug in conferring the Second Legion of Honor Award on Ninoy.

choice in public decision-making. It must therefore be guaranteed not only protection but existence, and must be allowed to speak freely and unafraid.

A FREE MEDIA, the most effective vehicle for untrammeled discussion, mutual criticism and refutation, is imperative if we are to prevent the entrenching of error.

A TRULY REPRESENTATIVE PARLIAMENT is a natural friend of liberty and an "unrestrained executive magistracy" is a natural enemy of freedom. The delicate system of checks and balances and the strict separation of powers are indispensable to a republican form of government.

UNDERDEVELOPMENT is the consequence of a capitalist system that perpetuates poverty and attendant human misery, of social structures based on gross inequalities in social well-being, privilege and power. This system must be replaced.

TYRANTS SUCCEED not because they are really strong but because the citizens are weak and indifferent. Threatened with various sanctions and "invitations to Crame," the intimidated masses cower in fear and supinely agree to pay for a false freedom with their basic civil liberties.

Only when a man has learned to fear nothing but the scruples of his conscience is he truly free. If he is ready to die, who can threaten him with death?

THE ESSENCE OF THE DEMOCRATIC FAITH is that through the continuing process of political education, men can become sufficiently reasonable to discover, with evidence and the give and take of free discussion, a better way of solving common problems.

THE PHILOSOPHY OF DEMOCRACY rests not on the belief in the natural goodness of man but his educability, not in the inevitability of social progress but in the potentialities of nature and intelligence.

IN THE END we get the government we deserve! No social or political organization can be better than the quality of the men and women who compose it. The quality of their lives will be determined by their visions, their courage and their fortitude.

GOVERNMENTS MAY SINK TO DEPTHS LOWER THAN THEIR SOURCE; THEY CANNOT RISE HIGHER!

"WE VOW

TO REMAIN STEADFAST, unintimidated, and to risk jail rather than see our liberties nibbled away.

TO SPEAK OUT AND DENOUNCE RAMPANT INJUSTICES. Justice can be realized only when "those who have not been victimized become as outraged as those who have been."

TO HELP OUR FELLOWMEN HELP THEMSELVES by removing the barriers of poverty, ignorance and disease that have stunted their growth for ages. Give them the tools and show them how best they can help themselves. A viable and a truly lasting revolution requires not only the overthrow of an oppressive external order but the continuing struggle for the minds, hearts and souls of men.

TO IMPOSE UPON OURSELVES the supreme obligation to crystallize and effectuate a determined and a committed OPPOSITION to the oppressive order, because tragedy of tragedies, we have become a nation with a history as dangerous to forget as it is painful to remember.

I grew up under a democratic capitalist system with its doctrines of free enterprise and *laissez faire*. Our economic system, copied from that of the United States, held out profit as the main motive force of economic activity. Profit is the great incentive. Capitalism appeals to the greed of men.

Capitalist doctrines went thusly: As much as possible, government must minimize its interference in matters of economics and business; governmental controls and regulations must be kept to the utmost minimum; the owners of business and industry must be allowed to fix the rules of competition.

But capitalism has not been all bad. History shows that it has been a vibrant, vital force.

Beginning with the 19th century, capitalism gave impetus to the growth of modern science and its application to daily life. It saw the triumphant assertion of individual daring, skill and enterprise over bureaucratic inertia and ineptitude. The ascendance of economic individualism brought with it a strengthening of political liberty.

But as the capitalist economy progressed, small economic units were gradually absorbed by the bigger enterprises that could afford the latest technological innovations. Access to credit and capital became a key to growth. Those who got it, or had the "access," grew, prospered, became the "signeurs" of the capitalist-dominated order.

True, work became collective. But ownership remained very individual. Thus the social phenomenon: the aristocracy of the moneyed few, the serfdom of the majority who are poor.

The challenge to capitalism was created by its failure as much as by its successes. Unemployment, for one thing, became a major problem. It demolished the myth that capitalism possessed a built-in, self-restoring natural harmony. For another, there was the contradiction between political freedom and economic dependence. This became more acute and accentuated with the growth of giant enterprises and the concentration of tremendous wealth in the hands of a few. Not content with making money, the new capitalists expanded into the field of media and politics. Politicians and journalists became like commodities—bought and sold in the open market!

The existence of industrial absolutism within the walls of political liberty, observes Prof. William Ebenstein, an eminent professor of politics, "lies at the basis of the critique of capitalism." He elaborates, "Whereas in a democracy political policies are arrived at through a process of consent that begins at the bottom and ends at the top, in corporate business economic policies are made from the top to the bottom."

And this was what handicapped Philippine democracy—from the start, it was a "capitalist democracy."

The dogma of *laissez faire* created a political situation that violated the canons of democracy. The owners of capital wielded powers so far-reaching—over their employees, over the public—without being accountable to the community, without being responsible to those whose fate they determined with their vital economic and political decisions. They were the country's plutocrats (they have been called 'oligarchs," which is a misnomer)—and plutocrats of the worst kind.

It is true that since the establishment of the Third Republic in 1946, there has been a substantial shift from pure free enterprise or *laissez faire* economy to a more government-regulated one. Currency controls were imposed in 1949, followed by import and export restrictions. Social security was established during the mid-fifties. Increasingly, with the establishment of the National Economic Council, central economic planning by government came to the fore.

During the late sixties and the early seventies, the concept of absolute property rights began to give way to a mere socialist concept of property. This concept—that property is a mere trust—even found a place in the 1973 Constitution.

But we are still a long way from freeing our economy from the tentacles of capitalism. Government financing institutions are still spawning overnight millionaires, just as they have done over the last five decades. I filed a bill in the Senate to limit government financing only to open corporations whose stocks are freely traded in the market. Closed family corporations, under my bill, would have to resort to private financing. It got nowhere.

Public mistrust in government-run businesses and industries continues to grow. And it is not surprising, because government planning is left to second- and third-rate minds who eventually penalize the whole economy with their half-baked economic concepts. Mediocrity is so prevalent in government because the better trained and experienced economic planners are pirated by private business after the government has spent much time and money on their education.

If central economic planning is to succeed, the private sector, instead of pirating government brains, must volunteer the services of their experts to the central planning agency. Only thus may the country operate as a national corporation dedicated to the welfare of all.

If I have taken great pains to elaborate on my personal ideology, it is because it grieves me profoundly to be carelessly branded a communist by those who never bothered to understand the difference between communism and Christian socialism. To them, socialism and communism are synonymous—a throwback to the McCarthyism of the early fifties in America. Unhappily, they are now the custodian of the New Morality.

VII

A Totalitarian Regime

> Fascism has learned from democracy the
> value of popular support for national
> policies, and it seeks to manufacture
> popular consent by a mixture of
> propaganda and terror.
>
> —PROF. WILLIAM EBENSTEIN

I N MY LAST appearance before Military Commission No. 2 last year,
I moved to quash the charges for violation of Republic Act No. 1700,
the Anti-Subversion Law. There were major flaws in the charge sheets,
I pointed out then. I shall do so again today.

I was served two sets of charge sheets. The first set, dated August 7, 1973, was
served on me on August 10, 1973. Later, those charge sheets were amended in
a second set dated August 14, 1973. This was served on me a few days later.

The amended charge sheets deleted the indicting phrase "to establish a totalitarian
regime." Like the first set, they did not assert positively that I was a communist
or a member of the Communist Party of the Philippines. Neither specified the
alien power that was supposed to "control and dominate" the Philippines after
a communist takeover.

The amendment was no small matter. It was basic and fundamental. Let us re-
examine it.

The charges were brought to my attention after I was eleven months in military detention, sometime in August 1973—eleven months after Mr. Marcos imposed martial rule and established in the Philippines a dictatorial rule, his totalitarian regime.

Now, the question: Why did the prosecutors amend the charge sheets, dropping the indicting clause, "the aim to set up a totalitarian regime," in the new set of charges? I advance: Because their own Commander-in-Chief, who ordered my prosecution, had in fact committed the very crime I was being charged with.

I ask: Who is guilty of subverting the Republic, of establishing a totalitarian regime—Mr. Marcos or I?

The framers of all our constitutions have repeatedly opted for a republican form of government. They have explicitly proscribed my monarchical or imperial tendencies. "The Philippines is a Republican State." (Art. II, Sec 1, 1973 Constitution)

With prescient realism, they viewed men as ambitious, corruptible if not corrupt, prone to unwise passions and foolish aspirations. To protect the people from the designs of the ambitious or the corruption of the venal, they designed a constitutional order based on a delicate system of checks and balances, a separation of powers and functions among the legislature, the executive and the judiciary. This basic tenet of democratic rule, the linchpin of our Republic, was designed, in the words of Justice Brandies, "not to promote efficiency but to preclude the exercise of arbitrary power."

Thus, all our constitutions—down to the contested 1973 Constitution—have affirmed the sovereignty of the people, that they shall govern by representation, that they shall live under a rule of law, not under the rule of any one man or any particular group of men. And their will can only be to live in a democracy, not suffer under a tyranny; a republican government, not a totalitarian regime.

The legislature was the engine of the Republic, enacting laws for the executive to execute—laws that empowered the executive to act but limiting the scope of its discretion. The executive commanded the sword, the armed forces; but the legislature controlled the purse, asking for and getting an accounting of how the taxes it authorized were spent by the executive. As a further "check," the legislature was constituted into a continuing inquest into the affairs of the executive—to ensure that the laws were faithfully carried out, to guard against corruption, usurpation and abuse of power by the executive.

But Mr. Marcos abolished Congress, our legislature, when he imposed martial rule. And he has refused to convene the *ad interim* National Assembly provided by the 1973 Constitution, the Constitution he "ratified."

CONTROL OF THE JUDICIARY

On September 22, 1972, Mr. Marcos established a totalitarian regime. On that fateful day, he proclaimed himself dictator. He issued General Order No. 1 which reads in part:

> NOW THEREFORE, I, FERDINAND E. MARCOS, President of the Philippines, by virtue of the powers vested in me by the Constitution as Commander-in-Chief of the Armed Forces of the Philippines, *do hereby proclaim that I shall govern the nation and direct the operation of the entire government, including all its agencies and instrumentalities,* and shall exercise all the powers and prerogatives appurtenant and incident to my position as such Commander-in-Chief of all Armed Forces of the Philippines. (Underlining supplied)

He placed his acts beyond the reach of the courts.
In General Order No. 3, issued on that September 22, 1972, Mr. Marcos decreed:

> I NOW HEREBY FURTHER ORDER that the Judiciary shall continue to function in accordance with its present organization and personnel, and shall try and decide in accordance with existing laws all criminal and civil cases, except the following:
>
> 1. *Those involving the validity, legality or constitutionality of any decree, order, or acts issued, promulgated or performed by me or by my duly designated representative pursuant to Proclamation 1081, dated September 21, 1972.* x x x" (Underlining supplied)

He completely destroyed the independence of the judiciary seven days after proclaiming martial rule. Judicial security of tenure was thrown into the dustbin of history.

On September 30, 1972, Mr. Marcos issued his now infamous Letter of Instructions No. 11, which reads as follows:

> "In order to facilitate the reorganization of the Executive Branch of the National Government as directed in Presidential Decree No. 1, dated September 24, 1972, and in order that the *Judicial Branch may also be reorganized* so as to meet the necessities of the present national emergency, make the government machinery more responsive to the needs of the people and effect economy, I hereby direct, pursuant to General Order No. 1, dated September 22, 1972, as amended, *that all officers of the national government whose appointments are vested in the President of the Philippines submit their resignations from office thru their department heads, not later than October 15, 1972."* (Underlining supplied)

The only officials exempted from this Letter of Instructions were the Chief Justice and associate justices of the Supreme Court, the Auditor General and the Chairman and members of the Commission on Elections. But the transitory provisions of the new Constitution—which was never legally ratified—took care of them, as we shall see shortly.

To complete his emasculation of the independence of the judiciary, Mr. Marcos decreed the Constitution proposed by the 1971 Constitutional Convention to be in force and in effect as of January 17, 1973, three months after his martial rule declaration, in Proclamation 1102.

No less than six of the ten justices of the Supreme Court said the new Constitution was not validly ratified. Contrary to what Proclamation 1102 claimed, the Supreme Court, in its resolution in the famous Javellana case, stated:

> On the second question of the validity of the ratification, Justices Makalintal, Zaldivar, Castro, Fernando, Teehankee and myself (Chief Justice Concepcion), or six (6) members of the Court, also hold that the Constitution proposed by the *1971 Constitutional Convention was not validly ratified* in accordance with Article XV, section 1 of the 1935 Constitution, which provides the only way for ratification, i.e., in an election or plebiscite held in accordance with law and participated in only by qualified and duly registered voters. (Josue Javellana, *et al* v. The Executive Secretary *et al*, GR. Nos. 1-36142, 36164, 36165, 36236; underlining supplied.)

In the opinion of Chief Justice Concepcion, the proposed Constitution "is not in force and effect; and that the 1935 Constitution is still the Fundamental Law of the Land." And he was joined by Justice Zaldivar, who pointed out:

> There can be no free expression, and there has been no expression, by the people qualified to vote all over the Philippines, of their acceptance or repudiation of the proposed Constitution under Martial Law.

And Justices Makalintal, Castro and Teehankee, on their part, found:

> Under a regime of martial law, with the free expression of opinion through the usual media restricted x x x there is no means of knowing, to the point of judicial certainty, whether the people have accepted the Constitution.

But Mr. Marcos, to complete his control of the judiciary, needed this new Constitution to legitimize his usurpations. Hence, he decreed it into existence.

The new Constitution's most controversial article is Article XVII, the so-called Transitory Provisions. These provisions reduced our judges and justices to the status of mere "casuals." Their security of tenure was abolished. To wit:

> *Sec. 9.* All officials and employees in the existing Government of the Republic

of the Philippines shall continue in office until otherwise provided by law or decreed by the incumbent President of the Philippines, but all officials whose appointments are by this Constitution vested in the Prime Minister shall vacate their respective offices upon the appointment and qualification of their successors.

Sec. 10. The incumbent members of the Judiciary may continue in office until they reach the age of seventy years, *unless sooner replaced in accordance with the preceding section hereof.* (Underlining supplied, 1973 Constitution)

DEATH OF PRESS FREEDOM

On that same September 22, 1972, Mr. Marcos killed press freedom in the Philippines. In his Martial Law Letter of Instructions No. 1, he ordered the secretaries of information and national defense:

> ...*you are hereby ordered forthwith to take over and control or cause the taking over of all such newspapers, magazines, radio and television facilities and all other media of communications,* wherever they are, for the duration of the present national emergency, or until otherwise ordered by me or by my duly designated representative. (Underlining supplied)

This tore away—in one stroke of the Marcos pen—the constitutional shield that safeguarded press freedom.

Freedom of the press, as we knew it—the people's right to know, the very bedrock of democracy—died with that martial law LOI#1. The independent *Manila Times* and its sister publications, echo chambers of the people's sentiments since the early American colonial rule, and the weekly magazine *Philippines Free Press,* always fearless and historically an unpleasant thorn in the side of those who governed, were closed by the martial law Brown Shirts at midnight of September 22, the first day of the Marcos martial rule.

Then, as if the "takeover" and "control" of the media by his secretaries of defense and information were insufficient still, Mr. Marcos penned General Order No. 19. Free speech is controlled effectively by GO# 19. It specifically prohibits the dissemination of false or scandalous remarks concerning the martial law government, its officers and its activities. It provides:

> Any person who shall utter, publish, distribute, circulate and spread rumors, false news and information and gossip...which tends to cause panic, divisive effects among the people, discredit or distrust the duly constituted authorities, undermine the stability of the government and the objectives of the New Society, endanger the public order, or cause damage to the interest or credit of the state x x x may be arrested or detained by authorities as having committed a crime against the security of the state. Penalty: at least six months in jail.

But these—LOI #1 and GO #19—were by Mr. Marcos' reckoning insufficient still. To complete the muzzling of the kept media, an unwritten decree was verbally transmitted to their editors—never picture the Marcos family in a bad light, they were told.

What Mr. Marcos has done is simply to control all news about himself, his wife, his family, his in-laws, his martial rule. How true is the sad commentary by those who yearn for the thunderous moral voices raised in our newspapers, radio and TV of pre-martial rule days: "Nothing can now be believed which appears in a newspaper."

Today, only those newspapers and affiliated radio-TV stations that are owned or controlled by the Marcos-Romualdez family—or by their cronies and hirelings who do the Marcoses' bidding with complete sycophancy—are allowed to operate the media. They are docile, never inquisitive, always ready to be "fed" the Palace line. Gone are the "snapshots of truth" given by the pre-martial law free press to the Filipino public.

Mr. Marcos' own later revelations are our evidence In *Notes on the New Society,* Mr. Marcos lets it be known:

> ...In late February and early March (1973), the summer plan of 1972 belatedly went into operation in Cotabato when *6,000 rebels overran most of the towns, threatening the IV Philippine Constabulary Zone headquarters in Parang as well as Cotabato City, destroyed the bridges and immobilized all transportation within the province. Before that, Basilan island was almost completely occupied by several thousand other rebels; Zamboanga del Sur was plunged into a state of turmoil. Again, before January, government troops had practically lost the province of Sulu,* except for the poblaciones (town proper), to numerically superior rebels and secessionists. (Marcos, *Notes,* pp. 107-108; underlining supplied)

These were never reported by the controlled press. What was reported was that the armed forces were doing great in the pacification campaign. The armed forces were always winning and the Muslim rebels were surrendering by the hundreds, per martial law press accounts. Indeed, the martial law media refused—as they still refuse—to report on the real events in Mindanao, Sulu and elsewhere.

But I am not surprised. After all, Mr. Marcos has defined their role in the New Society, his martial law Philippines. Journalists, Mr. Marcos has said, should be "committed agents of the government"—a role played, we once believed, only by newspapermen in totalitarian states. (Marcos quoted by Stanley Karnow, "An Alternative to Rhetoric," *Newsweek,* July 11, 1977, p. 33).

The role of the critical press has been assumed by the puny efforts of mimeograph operators spearheaded by the religious and—a heartening sight—by some college editors who refused to be cowed. Here, in their efforts, the people find the "snap-shots of truth."

They have risen to take up the moral responsibilities of those who have defaulted in the duty of the Fourth Estate as the public's conscience and voice. Inevitably, a number of them have had to pay the price of their courage. Here is what has happened, as reported by the International Commission of Jurists after a fact-finding inquiry by three ICJ missions in the Philippines:

> On December 5, 1976, *Sign of the Times* was closed by the Government, its equipment and documents impounded, and its leaders threatened with arrest and detention. On the same day, *The Communicator* suffered the same fate.

> On November 19 and 20, 1976, two church radio stations, DXBB in Malaybalay and DXCD in Tagum, were closed by military officials. Another station, DXBI in Basilan, was searched by military authorities on December 4 but was not closed.

> Other related incidents deserve mention here. One is the expulsion on November 2, 1976, of Arnold Zeitlin, for many years the *Associated Press* correspondent in Manila for having released from Manila 'false information concerning the Government.' Another was a denial on February 16, 1977, of an extension of the visa of Bernard Wideman, a respected correspondent of the *Far Eastern Economic Review* and the *Washington Post,* on the grounds that he was an undesirable alien whose presence would be inimical to the interests and security of the nation because of articles he had published concerning the Martial Law regime. Although his visa recently has been extended, the action of the government will undoubtedly have a chilling effect. There has been the recent expulsion by Philippine authorities of Catholic priests who have been active critics of the regime.

> More recently, we have been advised that on June 12, 1977, Philippine In-dependence Day, two newspaperwomen and a newspaperman were arrested by the Northern District Police Commander while covering an anti-Government rally of over 1,000 persons at St. Joseph's College in Quezon City. They were Marilyn Odehmar of the Japanese *Kyodo News Agency,* Nelly Sindayan of the Tokyo newspaper *Yomiuri Shimbun,* and Rey Palarca of *United Press International.* After a period of interrogation, they were released.

> Although some religious publications remain, such as *The Dialogue,* and although meetings are allowed to be held on a local basis from time to time, it can fairly be said that any substantial opposition by way of press, speech, demonstrations, or other expressions of opinion are and will continue to be sup-pressed by Philippine authorities so long as Martial Law continues. (ICJ Report, p. 27)

A free press and a truly representative parliament are indispensable to a republican form of government. Without these twin pillars of democracy, the peo-ple will not know what is going on. They will not be able to express to their representatives what they want.

A free press serves as a two-way conduit—through it, the people and their representatives communicate. If the people are deprived of a free press and cannot therefore make known their feelings and thoughts, their grievances and complaints, the representatives will not be able to correct the prevailing mistakes. In such a situation, democracy and government atrophy and wither.

A press that is not free has no value to the people. Indeed, it serves only to further their psychic conditioning to slavery!

OPPRESSION OF WORKINGMEN

Also on September 22, 1972, Mr. Marcos dealt the common people's freedoms a series of mortal blows. Organized labor was singled out for the most devastating blow. He outlawed strikes, the only potent weapon in the puny arsenal of the workingmen, and, as for the rest of the populace, he decreed as "strictly prohibited" any and all rallies, any and all demonstrations, any and all "other forms of group action"—under pain, for violators, of arrest and incarceration "for the duration of the national emergency." He ordered, in General Order No. 5:

> ...that henceforth and until otherwise ordered by me or by my duly designated representative, *all rallies, demonstrations and other forms of group actions* by persons within the geographical limits of the Philippines, *including strikes and pickets in vital industries* such as companies engaged in the manufacture or processing as well as in the distribution of fuel gas, gasoline, fuel or lubricating oil, in companies engaged in the production or processing of essential commodities or products for exports, and in companies engaged in banking of any kind, as well as in hospitals and in schools and colleges, *are strictly prohibited and any person violating this Order shall forthwith be arrested* and taken into custody and held for the duration of the national emergency or until he or she is otherwise ordered released by me or by my duly designated representative. (Underlining supplied)

Then, not satisfied with General Order No. 5, Mr. Marcos issued Presidential Decree No. 823, one of the most infamous decrees of his martial rule. It extended the prohibition on strikes "beyond essential industries" to include the entire spectrum of labor activity in the country.

The preamble claims a nationalistic purpose for the decree:

> ...the imposition of sufficient administrative controls over the activities of aliens and foreign organizations in the labor field, including the friends of the country whose concern for the welfare of the Filipino worker is deeply appreciated.

But its provisions have brought nothing but a brace of manacles on labor:

Ninoy being sworn in as Vice Governor of Tarlac.

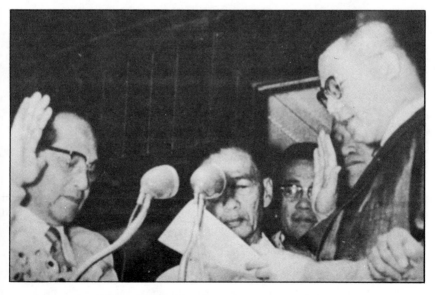

On February 3, 1961, President Carlos P. Garcia is shown swearing in Ninoy as Tarlac governor, being witnessed by former Governor Arsenio Lugay (center).

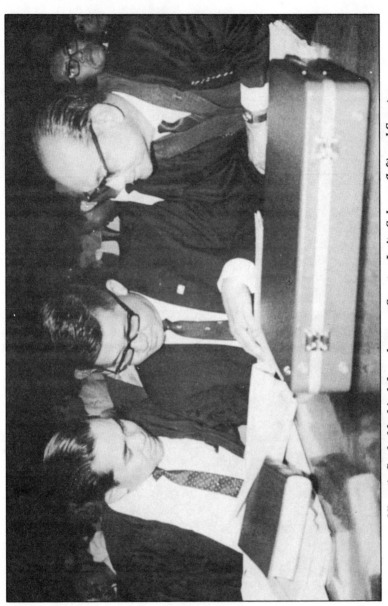

Ninoy is flanked by his defense lawyers, Senator Jovito Salonga (left) and Senator Estanislao Fernandez (right), who ably defended his underage status and got him a reprieve to continue his candidacy.

Section IV provides that union organizers can be arrested "on grounds of national security and public peace." Section VII prohibits all aliens and foreign organizations "from engaging directly or indirectly in all forms of trade union activities." Section VIII prohibits all forms of assistance to laborers or labor organizations "without the prior written permission of the Secretary of Labor."

Section IX provides for immediate and summary deportation and permanent debarment from re-entry to the Philippines as sanction for foreign violators of the decree. Section X gives the Secretary of Labor summary jurisdiction over unresolved labor disputes. Section XI provides incarceration of violators for the duration of the emergency. Section XII holds the decree applicable to *'all forms of farm tenants, rural workers and the like.'*

Some people speak with forked tongues. What we have in GO #5 and PD #823 belie the honeyed promises made by Mr. Marcos in proclaiming martial law: to "reform society," to give the Filipino workingman "labor justice," "social justice" and "sharing (of) the wealth" with the entrepreneurial class.

The New Society is "for the poor," he said in *Notes*. There will be, he pledged, "an authentic transformation of the social order." The "supreme criterion," he vowed, shall be: "How will it serve the cause of the rebellion of the poor?"

And detailing, he said: There will be no more "cynical exploitation of labor," there will be no more "amassing (of) profits with impunity." Because in such a situation, he explained, "economic development is irrelevant to the condition of the poor masses."

"The political authority will establish the priorities and provide the mechanisms of equalization," he said. "This is our social contract."

What gilded lies!

The simple truth is that what Mr. Marcos has done is to make good on another promise he made—little noticed, but there in the *Notes*—and this is: to remove "the strong disincentives to enterprise."

He has time and again proclaimed that his "constitutional authoritarianism" supports the free enterprise system. It aims, he says, to maximize economic development by attracting foreign capital to invest in Philippine industrial and tourism development.

Few can fault him his goal. The Philippines is a developing country, with a per capita income of less than $300 as of last year, 1977. The economy needs stimulation, and that, it seems, can come only from foreign investors. But at what price?

To this end—to make his martial law Philippines competitive with the other sweat shops of Asia—Mr. Marcos' come-ons are: GO #5, PD #823. And to complete his strategy of attraction, he has decreed a tight lid on wages!

The peso, as of October 1977, was worth only P0.5163 of what it was when Mr. Marcos imposed martial rule in 1972, according to the Central Bank's statistics. *(Business Day,* "Peso's Purchasing Power Down to P0.52," Dec. 6, 1977, p. 8). The peso's erosion is continuous—by 9.07 per cent in October last year from the previous October's, by 8.31 per cent this October from last year's—yet, as policy, per *Business day,* "the CB is not expected to take drastic steps.")

The Marcos decrees may have provided incentives to the elusive foreign investors. But, as various outraged sectors have noted, what cruel inequity the pro-investor, anti-labor Marcos package has imposed upon the Filipino workingmen!

The situation is so oppressive that, as the International Commission of Jurists missions found, "implementation of the decree has faced increasing opposition from organized labor and particularly from church groups interested in the rights of workers." Reports the ICJ:

> On November 8, 1975, the National Council of Churches in the Philippines passed a "Resolution on the Right of Labor to Strike."

> At the same time a letter, signed by Archbishop Jaime L. Sin of Manila and co-signed by 2,000 bishops, priests and members of religious orders, protesting Decree No. 823, was sent to the President.

> A similar letter was sent to the President signed by Archbishop Antonio Mabutas of Davao and bishops Joseph Regan, Carlos van Ouivelant and Fernando Capella.

> On November 16, 1975, the priests and religious of the diocese of Imus issued a declaration protesting the decree.

> In the Manila area, a Committee of Christians for Justice and Human Rights was formed for the same purpose.

> Opposition to the decree reached a crescendo on December 6, 1975, when 6,000 people assembled at the Plaza Miranda (on the day when President Ford was visiting Manila) to demonstrate their opposition to the ban on the right of labor to strike for just wages and conditions of employment.

The ICJ Report noted that the Philippine government is a signatory to the International Covenant on Economic, Social and Cultural Rights, Article 8 of which asserts the right of labor to strike, and pointedly concluded that PD #823 is "a violation of the Philippine government's obligation under the Covenant."

It has been a strategy of carrots for the investors, the martial law stick for the Filipino workingmen!

RIGGED REFERENDA

Mr. Marcos has been trying to justify his continued one-man rule on the ground that the Filipino people have endorsed his power-grab in four so-called referenda. What they in fact are: rigged referenda, much like Hitler's were. "A farce," the *New York Times'* Tillman Durdin called the first one in 1973.

And as late as July 28, 1977, when the International Commission of Jurists issued its report, *The Decline of Democracy in the Philippines,* after sending three fact-finding missions to the Philippines, the ICJ finding was: "These referenda cannot be considered, in any way, as a true measure of the will of the people."

In fact, after intensive and extensive inquiries, what the ICJ missions singularly found was: the Marcos referenda, like the "ratification" of the 1973 Constitution, were each an unacceptable anomaly. Each was, they concluded, clearly and demonstrably, a false representation of the Filipino people's political will—done, the Report said, with "a substantial element of intimidation" while "military forces dominate."

"The technique of the use of referenda to justify or legitimize the perpetuation of personal power is not without precedent in modern society," the ICJ Report observed, citing Park Chung Hee's resort to it in South Korea "to give the imprimatur of public approval to his dictatorship." In the wake of the Marcos referenda, the Report said, the ICJ missions found that:

1. Martial law is in effect.

2. Free public debate is prohibited.

3. Political opponents are in jail and some have been tortured and maltreated.

4. There is no free press, radio or television.

5. The public media, especially television and radio, are used only as instruments of government propaganda.

6. There is no freedom of assembly.

7. Military forces dominate the nation.

8. The secrecy of the ballot is not preserved, with the inevitable effect of a substantial element of intimidation.

9. The counting and evaluation of the voting is done by government nominees.

10. The issues presented are framed by the government in a manner likely to achieve a certain response.

11. There is limited judicial review and no legislative control.

Under these conditions and circumstances, the results of these referenda cannot be considered, in any way, as a true measure of the will of the people. (ICJ Report, p. 19)

No greater injury has been done the Filipino than by these referenda. Each not only tightens the chains he has worn since September 21, 1972, but makes him morally benumbed, callous, indifferent—makes him share the guilt, kills his conscience!

Broken, silent, emptied of their guts, Filipinos are made to go through the personally demeaning process of voting "Yes, Marcos, be President, Prime Minister, Speaker, Commander-in-Chief, Martial Law Authority, Autocrat for Life—and Beyond!" And they vote, "Yes *na* yes!"

No other act parades before them—and the world—their debilitating captivity!

It has been a personally distasteful experience. But Filipinos can refuse to participate in the charade only if they find once more "the valor that resides in the man himself and his will to endure." The penalty is, as Mr. Marcos has decreed: six months in the martial law prisons.

It sickens many, I'm sure. But few dare risk the reprisals of the martial law custodians—and they can be really repressive. The International Commission of Jurists has documented: "Andrew Ocampo was arrested on October 17, 1976, apparently for being in possession of referendum literature , despite the decree ensuring freedom of discussion; he was subjected to water cure and electric-shock treatment"; "Willie Tatania was arrested during the referendum period of October 1976 by agents of M-2 and subjected to electric shock and strangulation, was kept incommunicado through one month in a safehouse code-named 'Shera Hotel'."

Because I refused to participate in his referenda, I have been penalized by my military jailors. I was "punished" for my refusal.

In 1976, when Mr. Marcos announced the holding of his fourth referendum to "amend" the Constitution he declared "ratified" in 1973, I formally challenged him to a nationwide radio-TV debate on the basic issue—his call upon the people to make him President-Premier for life. I wrote him:

"Mr. Ferdinand E. Marcos
Malacañang, Manila

Thru: *The Commanding General
Philippine Army*

Sir:

I have been informed that you have authorized the Commission on Elections to invite former Senator Raul Manglapus to come back to the Philippines under a guaranteed safe-conduct pass and participate in the public debates on the issues involved in the coming October 16 referendum-plebiscite.

Two weeks ago, I was also informed, you told members of the Manila Rotary

Club that you have been missing the rough and tumble of political debates.

You do not have to wait for Mr. Manglapus to return nor is it necessary for you to go abroad to find opposition to your martial law regime. I am ready and willing to debate with you and I do not need any safe-conduct pass. All I ask is that I be allowed to speak freely.

So that the nation can profit from it, may I suggest that you order a full radio-TV coverage and that the debate be held in that traditional and historic forum of our people: Plaza Miranda.

In the crucible of our debate, you can tell our people about the so-called achievements of martial law. I am prepared to tell our people the simple truth about its reality.

The fact that I am a detainee—on your own orders—should not disqualify me from debating with you. Both the old and the new Constitutions provide that I am presumed innocent until found guilty by a competent, independent and impartial tribunal.

So that our people may know the whole truth about martial law, I trust you will not deny them this opportunity to hear both sides of the question—your side and the side of one who can speak about it out of his own experience.

Yours truly,

BENIGNO S. AQUINO, JR.
Fort Bonifacio
October 1, 1976"

For my effrontery, all my visiting privileges were cancelled two weeks after I sent him my letter of challenge. Even my lawyers were not allowed to visit me for four months.

I was held completely incommunicado from October 14 to November 27, 1976. My family was allowed to visit me only on November 27—and only because it was my birthday. My visiting privileges continued to be suspended until about two weeks before Christmas.

What was I about to tell Mr. Marcos and the people? I was going to say:

1. The amending process proposed by Mr. Marcos was unconstitutional—patently unconstitutional. Only the interim National Assembly, under the 1973 Constitution he "ratified," could amend the Constitution or call a constitutional convention.

2. Mr. Marcos' amendments would do away with the constitutional provision for the interim National Assembly and create, in its place, a Batasang Pamban-

sa, a People's Assembly of 120 members, consisting of "elected" regional representatives on a proportional basis (the formula has yet to be announced) plus the
members of the Marcos cabinet to be appointed to the Batasan by Mr. Marcos.

3. The Batasang Pambansa would have the same powers as the interim National Assembly provided by the 1973 Constitution as parliamentary replacement
to the Congress killed by Mr. Marcos when he imposed martial rule, but the
power to ratify treaties would be divested from it. Only Mr. Marcos' signature
would be needed to ratify treaties.

4. Mr. Marcos alone would be empowered to convene the Batasang Pambansa. He could take his time doing it, because no time limit was set for him to
convoke the Batasan under the amendments. In fact, he could choose not to convoke the Batasan, at all, as he never convened the interim National Assembly.

5. The offices of President, Prime Minister and Speaker of the Batasang Pambansa would be merged in Mr. Marcos' person—in Mr. Marcos himself,
personally—to be assumed by him without any vote by the Batasan.

6. As President-Premier-Speaker, Mr. Marcos alone would have the sole power
to determine the disqualification of cabinet members. He may change them at
any time.

7. Mr. Marcos, as President-Premier-Speaker, would have the power to legislate
by decree even after the lifting of martial law if he felt—he alone would determine this—the Batasang Pambansa was not doing its job. In effect, there would
be two legislatures—Mr. Marcos and the People's Assembly.

Religious leaders, educators, former politicians and the libertarian youth raised
a howl. The referendum nevertheless was held as scheduled. As expected, Mr.
Marcos got all the amendments he sought by a staggering 90.5% of the votes "cast."

It was a flagrant non-system of non-election, the way the Filipinos allegedly
voted to keep their chains for the remainder of Mr. Marcos' life. It was so incredible, so implausible, so unbelievable, what those referenda yielded—especially when
we recall:

*Two weeks before martial law, the Gallup Poll released a survey, published
by the *Manila Chronicle*, showing Mr. Marcos' popular acceptance rating down
to an all-time low of 21%; and,

*His own testimony, made in his *Notes on the New Society,* that when he imposed martial law, the government was "weak," his administration was almost...im-
mobilized," and he "knew, in the first place, that the political opposition was confident about the national elections, which were merely fourteen months away."
(Marcos, *Notes,* pp. 3-4).

Against this background must be seen the 95.27% show of hands "ratification"
of the 1973 Constitution pronounced by Mr. Marcos a bare four months after he
instituted his martial rule, the 90.67% "vote" he claimed he won in July 1973
to "continue beyond 1973," and the other referenda of self-perpetuation that

followed.

NO JUSTIFICATION FOR MARTIAL LAW

In issuing its report *The Decline of Democracy in the Philippines,* the International Commission of Jurists, composed of the world's leading jurists, explained that its missions were unable to examine in any detail the circumstances existing at the time of the proclamation of martial law in the Philippines in September 1972. The missions, the ICJ Report said, merely accepted the Supreme Court's position that the circumstances justified the imposition of martial law "at that time."

But after five years—the Report was released on July 28, 1977, on the eve of the so-called World Law Conference subsidized by the martial law regime in Manila—the ICJ concluded:

> We are, however, unable to accept that such circumstances still exist today, so as to justify the continuance of martial law throughout the country, still less to justify the measures taken within, including the suspension of Parliament and all political activity, severe restrictions on all basic civil liberties, prolonged detention without trial of political opponents, and the *substitution of military tribunals for the normal civilian process.*

x x x

> Martial law in the Philippines is now in its fifth year. The executive rules by decree. There is no legislature, no elections, and very little judicial review. The people are not allowed to choose their representatives. Citizens languish in jail without charge, many since martial law was declared. *Military authority is supreme.*

x x x

> The present government is now employing the power granted it by the Constitution not primarily to protect the nation from "invasion, insurrection, or rebellion, or imminent danger thereof, when the public safety requires it" but rather *to perpetuate the personal power of the President and his collaborators and increase the power of the military to control Philippine society."*

x x x

> *The referendum of October 16, 1976, marked the end of democracy in the Philippines by giving the power to the President to suspend the legislature and to rule indefinitely by decree.* (Underlining supplied)

The ICJ Report conceded there might yet be need to continue martial law in the Mindanao area "where there is evidence of a threat to the security of the nation." But continuing martial rule in the other parts of the country, it said, has brought the ICJ to the inescapable conclusion that it is but an instrument for *"perpetuation of his (Marcos') personal power."* It supported its conclusion thus:

1. The flow of foreign-manufactured war materials into the Philippines appears to have ceased. Over 600,000 weapons have been seized by the authorities since Martial Law.

2. Although President Marcos frequently refers in general terms to the Communist threat, it is believed that there is no longer a serious threat of an armed overthrow of the Government by the Communist Party, still less that the suppression of civil and political liberties is necessary in order to combat it. The breakdown of law and order from the throwing of bombs in public places to other acts of terrorism has ceased.

3. The New People's Army is no longer an effective force threatening the life of the nation. Most of the leadership has surrendered or been arrested. The highest estimate of the membership is 20,000, but this is a nominal figure, as the armed force is not numbered above 1,000 and this force is largely contained within the mountains and is not able to operate effectively in populated areas.

4. The various "private armies" of the old-time politicians and oligarchs have been virtually eliminated.

5. There have been no serious incidents of armed rebellion except in Mindanao, where the Moro National Liberation Front continues to negotiate for its rights and where approximately 6,000 rebels are adequately contained by the Philippine Army. (ICJ Report, pp. 11-12)

And to impress unequivocally upon the Marcos martial law regime that it had been found blatantly wanting in the field of human rights, the ICJ wrote into the report on the Philippines the "necessary safeguards (for citizen rights) under martial law" which it had drawn up in its spring meeting in Vienna in April 1977. The report urged:

Where a state of siege or martial law is declared to deal with an exceptional situation the following basic safeguards should be strictly observed:

1. Arrests and detentions, particularly administrative detentions, *must be subject to judicial control and remedies, such as habeas corpus or amparo, must always be available to test the legality of any arrest or detention.* The right of every detainee to legal assistance by a lawyer of his choice must at all times be recognized. The holding of suspects in solitary confinement should be strictly limited in accordance with law.

2. *Effective steps must be taken to prevent torture and ill-treatment of detainees.* When it occurs, those responsible must be brought to justice. *All detention centers, prisons and camps for internment of detainees must be subject to judicial con-*

trol. Delegates of accredited international organizations should have permission to visit them.

3. Illegal or unofficial forms of *repression practiced by paramilitary or parapolice groups must be ended and their members brought to justice.*

4. The *jurisdiction of military tribunals should be strictly limited to offenses by the armed forces. Civilians should not be tried in military tribunals.*

5. The *independence of the judiciary and of the legal profession should be fully respected.* The right and duty of lawyers to act in the defense of political prisoners, as of other prisoners, and their immunity for action taken within the law in defense of their clients should be fully recognized and respected. (Underlining supplied)

Indeed, the ICJ Report's conclusions were a bill of particulars against the Marcos martial rule. *"The Philippine government, using military authority,"* the Report said, *"has denied the Philippine people their basic rights under the Constitutions of 1935 and 1973."* It pointed out that the martial regime:

(a) has *denied to the people of the Philippines their basic right freely to elect their own governmental representatives in the manner provided by their own Constitutions;*

(b) has *effectively abolished the right of habeas corpus;*

(c) *has abolished the freedom of the press* by seizing and closing down all newspapers, periodicals, and magazines which in any way, directly or indirectly, oppose the policies of the government;

(d) has *seriously inhibited freedom of speech and information by* arresting and detaining many of those who oppose the Government. Although a few Opposition leaders are allowed to continue to appear in public, they do not have access to the media. They are allowed this limited freedom of operation for public relations purposes and because they present no serious threat to the rule of the Executive;

(e) has *effectively abolished the right of the laborer to strike* for better wages and working conditions;

(f) has *not yet taken effective steps to prevent the use of torture* by security units of the Philippine military establishment when interrogating suspects. These interrogations, usually held at the private offices of the security units themselves or at 'safehouses' (private homes taken over by security officers for interrogation purposes), last for days and even months. The methods of torture employed within the last eighteen months include water treatment, electric-shock, 'boxing,' prolonged isolation, threats, and in the case of women, carried out while naked under humiliating and degrading conditions...;

(g) has *detained without charge of trial several hundred detainees, some for as long as five years.* The Government admits that it still has 4,000 detainees, of which 1,400 are so-called 'subversive detainees.' It is estimated that approximately 250 of these have been held for many years and that the balance is a floating population which changes from time to time depending on the frequency of arrests and releases;

It is to be noted that *there is no legislation under Martial Law which authorizes detention without trial. However, by the simple expedient of not bringing cases to trial, suspects, whether or not charged, have been and still are being detained in this way for years, and the courts have done nothing to prevent this process or expedite the cases;*

(h) *has in this way used the device of 'preliminary investigation' to impose prolonged detention without trial.* Many detainees have been in 'preliminary detention' for years and have not been charged at all;

(i) has *severely limited the Filipino's right to leave and to return to his country.* (ICJ Report, pp. 43-44; underlining supplied)

Pointedly addressing itself directly to the Marcos martial law regime, the ICJ Report called on it—*"in order to ensure the better protection of the rights of its citizens*—to give consideration at an early date" to:

terminating Martial Law, at least over the greater part of the country;

granting *amnesty to all detainees* suspected of subversive or seditious activities who are not charged with complicity in any act of violence;

terminating the power of military courts to try civilians and transferring all pending cases to the civilian courts;

calling the interim National Assembly followed by general elections provided for in the 1973 Constitution. (ICJ Report, pp. 44-45; underlining supplied)

Additionally, the ICJ Report called on Mr. Marcos to:

(a) Institute effective supervisory procedures *to ensure that the use of torture by military security officers when interrogating suspects ceases.*

(b) *Discontinue the use of safehouses as temporary detention centers* and transfer all arrested persons, within twenty-four hours of arrest, to prisons or military prison camps, from which they should not thereafter be removed for purposes of interrogation.

(c) Accelerate all cases now held by the military authorities by completing preliminary charges against all detainees within three months. All detainees not charged within that time should be released.

(d) Bring into effect Article XII of the Constitution providing for an ombudsman. A well-respected jurist, not in the employ of the Government, should be appointed to this office.

(e) Enhance the economic, social, and cultural rights of Philippine citizens in the areas of land reform, housing, education, etc.

(f) *Terminate the ban on the right to strike* without delay.

(g) *Restore freedom of the press and association and discontinue* the policy of expelling journalists and priests.

(h) *Restore the independence of the judiciary* by proper assurances, the return of all letters of resignation of judges, and the enactment of legislation guaranteeing the life appointment of Justices of the Supreme Court.

(i) Finally, *appoint a Commission to study and recommend how the state of Martial Law, already in existence for nearly five years, can be dismantled and the state returned to a liberal democracy* as provided for in both the 1935 and the 1973 Constitution. (ICJ Report, p. 45; underlining supplied)

The 45-page ICJ Report—released only after a third fact-finding mission was sent to the Philippines in February 1977 to supplement the first two missions in 1975—was signed by Mr. William Butler, U.S. chairman of the ICJ executive committee and head of the missions; Mr. John P. Humphrey of Canada, eminent professor of law and former director of the Human Rights Division of the United Nations for two decades; and Mr. G.E. Bisson of New Zealand.

Upon his return to Canada from his Manila trip, Professor Humphrey told the Associated Press in an interview: "There are serious violations of human rights in the Philippines." I can tick off practically every paragraph of the Declaration of Human Rights and say that this is being violated in the Philippines. He then announced his resignation as chairman of the Committee on Human Rights of the Manila World Law Conference. He did not wish, he said, to preside over what he felt would be "a whitewashing operation."

Predictably, Mr. Marcos denounced the ICJ Report as "politically motivated." He did not explain why.

MARCOS, DIKTADOR!

They fell in rapid succession: Mr. Marcos' mortal blows on freedom. And when he was done, we were left with—a totalitarian regime, with Mr. Marcos as dictator!

Breaking his silence on Mr. Marcos' usurpations, former President Macapagal, Mr. Marcos' immediate predecessor and president of the 1971 Constitutional Convention, categorically stated in his book, *Democracy in the Philippines:* "Martial law is a pretext to enable President Marcos to indefinitely rule over our country beyond his constitutional term with despotic power."

No question about it: in Mr. Macapagal's considered opinion, the Marcos martial rule is illegal, unconstitutional and illegitimate. The legitimate purpose of martial law, he stressed, is primarily to maintain public safety and public order. Once peace and order is established, the continuation of martial law becomes a patently unconstitutional act and, in Mr. Marcos' case, a usurpation of the Presidency. He asked: Did not Mr. Marcos, on September 19, 1973, proclaim that "the crisis of survival has been overcome"?

As to Mr. Marcos' other reason for imposing martial law—the reform of Filipino society to establish a New Society—the former President pointedly observed: It is beyond the scope and cannot be a valid purpose of martial law, "because by its nature, it (the project of a New Society) is of indefinite duration." He concluded with the indictment:

> The fact that the building of a "New Society" was made an aim of martial law shows that the proclamation was not for the purpose of coping with communist subversion; that dealing with communist rebels was a convenient justification for the installation of a dictatorship.

Mr. Macapagal, in his book, shared the opinion of many of the nation's legal and constitutional luminaries: Mr. Marcos, his successor in the Presidency, has exceeded the bounds of the Constitution. "Among other unconstitutional acts" he ticked off, "he (Marcos) has disregarded and later abolished Congress, bypassed the Judiciary, and issued decrees in the nature of law."

What are the hallmarks of a totalitarian regime? I have drawn up a checklist and indicated how the Marcos government fits the description:

1. Concentration of all the awesome powers of government in one man. Mr. Marcos has done this!

2. Abolition or bypassing of Parliament or Congress. Mr. Marcos has done this!

3. Emasculation of the Judiciary. Mr. Marcos has done this!

4. Abolition of the free press. Mr. Marcos has done this! Worse, he not only controls but owns, through his relatives and cronies, all the major newspapers, radio and TV networks of the nation today!

5. Banning of political parties. Outlawing of strikes. Suspension of the right to peaceably assemble. Mr. Marcos has done these!

6. Police state brutality and repression. Mr. Marcos has ordered or at least tolerated this! No less than Amnesty International, the prestigious guardian of human rights all over the world, has denounced the long detention without trial of numerous Filipinos, the use of systematic torture, and the wanton inhumanity to their fellowmen by Mr. Marcos' martial law minions. In the Marcos martial rule, Amnesty International has charged, evidence is "literally tortured into existence."

n outright crowd favorite, Ninoy as last speaker during the wee hours of the orning in the 1969 presidential campaign.

ioy delights his audience by reading excerpts from the book of his political al.

Ninoy announcing refusal to take part in proceedings of "Kangaroo Court",
August 27, 1973.

VIII

EVIDENCE TORTURED
INTO EXISTENCE

It is mockery of justice to send someone
to a concentration camp, to hold him
there without legal process.

— POPE PIUS XII

The future of the Republic, to a great
extent, depends upon our maintenance
of justice pure and unsullied.

— JUSTINIAN

AMNESTY International in its annual report says:

> The mission interviewed 105 prisoners held in detention centers. Of those in-
> terviewed, 68 informed the delegates that they had been subjected to brutal treat-
> ment, which in most cases took place when they were under interrogation for
> varying periods following their arrest. (Amnesty International Report, 22 Nov
> - 5 Dec 1975, p. 7)

Time in its cover story on "Torture" (August 16, 1976) carried Amnesty International's report. AI's findings, *Time* observed, corroborated an earlier report by
the Association of Major Religious Superiors of the Philippines on torture of detainees by the Marcos regime. But to the dismay of the Religious Superiors, Mr.

Marcos vehemently denied that torture was martial law SOP or policy. He assured them that what they found were "aberrations."

If it was not SOP or policy, if the acts of savage, brutal and sadistic torture of Marcos martial law political prisoners were "aberrations," one is led to either of two conclusions, seeing as how the "aberrations" have persisted:

1) Mr. Marcos was lying, which he has admitted in *Notes* he has done occasionally to smooth out ruffled feelings, at least in his relationships with the family of his then Vice-President, Fernando Lopez; or,

2) Mr. Marcos has lost control over his Brown Shirts, which is a worse situation — worse for him and far worse for the Filipinos.

Their "unavoidable conclusion," AI's investigators reported, "was that torture was used freely and with extreme cruelty, often over long periods." They itemized the torture methods employed commonly by Mr. Marcos' PC, NISA, ISAFP and other investigation/intelligence outfits:

1. Electric shock - a small electric generator is used and wires are attached to the genitals of the detainees;

2. Lying-on-the-air torture, otherwise known as San Juanico Bridge. The individual is made to lie with his feet on one bed and his head on a second bed, and is beaten and kicked whenever he lets his body fall or sag.

3. Truth serum - administered by some doctors at the V. Luna General Hospital.

4. Russian roulette - a revolver with one bullet in the cylinder is placed on the head of a detainee and the trigger is squeezed.

5. Falanga - beating of the soles of the feet till the detainee is unable to walk.

6. Beating with fists, kicks and karate blows.

7. Beating with a variety of contusive instruments, including rifle butts, heavy wooden clubs and family-size soft drink bottles.

8. Heads are pounded against walls or furniture (such as the edge of a filing cabinet).

9. Standing naked before an air-conditioning unit turned on full blast or made to sit on a block of ice; and

10. Water cure and other forms of water torture. (AI Report, page 10)

The AI Report revealed that while torture was apparently not so widespread among women detainees, "intimidation involving threats of sexual assault was commonplace."

On violations and utter disregard of civil rights by the Marcos martial law regime, the AI Report noted:

Unhappily, the Amnesty International Mission *collected overwhelming evidence that these promises and guarantees (civil rights), at least up to the time of the mission, were meaningless nullities for persons detained under suspicion for political offenses.* As set forth elsewhere in this report, the evidence establishes *a consistent pattern of gross violations of internationally recognized human rights,* including systematic and severe torture, and cruel, inhuman and degrading treatment during the interrogation process; indefinite detention, in many cases for several years, without being informed of the charges and without trial of the issues; a systematic denial of the right to bail on the grounds that suspension of the privilege of the writ of HABEAS CORPUS suspends the right to bail; and other flagrant violations of the rights which are said to be 'enshrined' in the Bill of Rights." (AI Report pp. 81-82; underlining supplied)

The most damning portion of the AI Report deals with its observations on the judicial system under the Marcos martial law regime. I quote it in full to do it justice:

iv. *THE JUDICIAL SYSTEM*

Spokesmen for the Government of the Philippines have called the martial law system a form of 'constitutional authoritarianism,' arguing that in spite of the abolition of the legislative branch of government, the judiciary, and particularly the Supreme Court, provide an effective 'constitutional' check on arbitrary action. *The short answer to this argument is the overwhelming evidence of widespread systematic torture and prolonged detention without trial or even formal charges — no court in the Philippines, including the Supreme Court has taken effective action to prevent these massive violations of human rights.*

The critical flaw in this argument, however, is that under the terms of sections 9 and 10 of the Transitory Provisions, members of the judicial branch, including *Justices of the Supreme Court, are subject to removal at any time by Presidential decree, thus, stripping them of the independence which the principle of tenure is intended to guarantee.* Furthermore, there has been, by decree, a massive shift of jurisdiction from civil courts to military commissions, particularly offenses which are political in nature, and the only appeal from judgments of military commissions is through the Secretary of National Defense to the President. Thus, the Supreme Court's theoretical ability to provide a constitutional check on arbitrary executive action has been drastically reduced. Finally, within days after the declaration of martial law, President Marcos, in Letter of Instruction number 11, directed all lower Court officers to submit undated letters of resignations, and the President has since not hesitated to use that power in forcing the resignations of a number of judges.

In sum, stripped of its jurisprudence and its independence, the judiciary of the Philippines has become totally ineffective in preventing the violations of human rights detailed in this report. *The rule of law under martial law is authoritarian presidential-military rule unchecked by constitutional guarantees or limitations.* (Amnesty International Report, pp. 81-82; underlining supplied)

The AI Mission said that in case after case, in country after country, it found that suspension of the privilege of the Writ of Habeas Corpus (or of analogous processes designed to provide some outside judicial scrutiny of the legality of detention within a reasonable time after arrest) tended to create the pre-condition of torture.

The AI Report said:

> Within three years of the suspension of the writ and the declaration of martial law, the Republic of the Philippines, as of the time of the Amnesty International mission, has *been transformed from a country with a remarkable tradition to a system of Star Chamber methods which have been used on a wide scale to literally torture evidence into existence.* (AI Report, p. 85; underlining supplied)

The AI Mission found out, in many interviews, that detainees were tortured till they agreed to falsely testify against themselves and against people whom they did not even know. To escape further torture, they signed not only false confessions condemning themselves but also false affidavits incriminating other people. And to cap it all, they were forced to sign affidavits "swearing to the fact" that they had not been maltreated — that they were in good health, that their "confessions" were given freely, voluntarily and without threats or intimidation.

Concluding their detailed report, the Amnesty International delegates pointedly recommended to Philippine authorities the immediate stoppage of torture of detainees, the re-establishment of an independent judiciary, the restoration of the Writ of Habeas Corpus "to reassure those who respect the fine traditions enshrined in the 1935 Philippine Constitution and promised in the new Constitution."

These recommendations are precisely the reason for my struggle.

The AI Report named names: not only the torture victims, but the torturers, mostly officers of the Philippine Constabulary (PC), the National Intelligence and Security Agency (NISA), other military and police intelligence agencies. Safehouses where tortures were conducted were pinpointed.

This report is now being circulated among the 150 member-nations of the United Nations. It is not only the most telling and most damning indictment of the Marcos martial law regime, it is one of the most shaming documents on Philippine affairs.

Mr. Marcos, in a radio-TV address to the Filipino nation on December 11, 1974, emphatically stated, "*No one, but no one, has been tortured.*" Then, when he was confronted with incontrovertible evidence, he changed his tune, affirming what he could not deny but calling these "aberrations." In the case of Miss Trining Herrera, he even ordered the court martial of one 1st Lt. Eduardo Matillano and one 2nd Lt. Prudencio Regis, Jr.: he had no choice, it seemed, because Trining's denunciation of torture inflicted upon her was taken up directly by the U.S. government.

Lt. Matillano and Lt. Regis were acquitted promptly by a Marcos court martial. With this, the Herrera case was officially put to rest — raised officially again only by Justice Cecilia Muñoz Palma who, in one of the World Law Conference's panel discussions, questioned the fairness of the military tribunal's handling of the charges and peremptory acquittal of the two military officers.

But Trining Herrera's case is not the only "aberration." There are many others — some catalogued by the Religious Superiors, others reported by Amnesty International, others itemized by the International Commission of Jurists, still others unknown by anyone, excepting the tortured and their torturers. Let us cite some cases:

*Rev. CESAR TAGUBA, a Protestant pastor: Arrested 3 March 1974 in Quezon City. He was taken by Capt. Esguerra of ISAFP to a house in Marikina. In the house *he was handed a gun and asked to commit suicide.* The gun was placed against his temple and he pulled the trigger six times, but there were apparently no bullets in the gun. *He was beaten with fists and asked questions,* to which he did not reply. *After two days he collapsed from the beatings.*

He was kept at the "safe house" in Marikina for two weeks. *As a result of the beatings, part of a front tooth was broken.* On one occasion, the leg of a chair was pressed on to his hand on the floor. *He was denied food for three days and forced to drink his own urine.*

After further beatings, *he looked so unwell that he was taken to V. Luna Hospital where he was placed in the psychiatric ward.* He said his interrogators asked for 'truth serum' to be used on him, but the doctor involved argued against it because it could have harmed him permanently.

He remained in the hospital until May 1974, when the National Council of Churches of the Philippines began searching for him. Following representations by the Protestant Churches, of which he is a pastor, the Rev. Cesar Taguba was transferred to Ipil, and later on 15 August 1974 he was transferred to YRC.

He was charged under Article 147 of the Revised Penal code for "illegal association." He had not been formally charged. (Amnesty International Report, p. 50; underlining supplied).

JOSE LACABA, 30, a newspaperman, and BONIFACIO ILAGAN, 24, a student: Arrested 25 April 1974 in Baliwag, Bulacan. *Both were beaten immediately upon arrest. Gun barrels were struck into their stomachs, they were pushed to the floor, trodden on, kicked, and hit on the back of their heads with rifle butts. They were taken to 5 CSU office in Camp Crame and tortured the whole day.* Lt. Rodolfo Aguinaldo and Sgt. Narciso Cervantes interrogated Ilagan, while Lacaba was interrogated by Capt. Ocampo, a man named Crispin of 5 CSU's Special Mission Group (SMG), Dagasdas, and Sgt. Cervantes. In addition, passing 5 CSU staff struck the prisoners.

They were struck on the body with punches, karate chops and kicks. Lacaba was forced into a squatting posture and was then beaten on the shins with a rattan instrument. Both were subjected to the "higa sa hangin" (lying-on-the-air) treatment, also known as San Juanico Bridge. In this form of torture, the victim is made to lie down with his head resting on the edge of one cot, his feet on the edge of another cot, his arms straight and stiff at his side, and his body "hanging like the bridge" between the two cots. Both prisoners were forced to maintain this position despite falling repeatedly. *All the interrogators, as well as others, continued to strike them with punches and kicks.*

On another occasion, Lacaba was questioned by Lt. Poblete of 5 CSU. Lacaba was made to close his eyes; then a hand that he presumed to be Poblete's rhythmically slapped his eyes and the nape of his neck. In another instance, Lacaba was kicked in the chest by Sgt. Ricardo, was jabbed in the ribs by Dagasdas and two SMG soldiers. On one occasion he was taken to Victoriano Luna Hospital in Metro Manila and *injected with what he described as "truth serum," which he said made him talk drunkenly.*

Both men were *kept incommunicado for over two months,* while their relatives had to go from office to office to try to obtain permission to visit. *The persistent brutal treatment of both prisoners continued for seven months* after their arrest and since January 1975, it became relatively less intensive.

Lacaba, aged 30, is a journalist, was formerly staff writer of the *Free Press* and the executive editor of *Asia-Philippines Leader.* Ilagan, aged 24, was a former student of the University of the Philippines. Both men said that they were involved in an "underground" publication which opposed the imposition and administration of martial law because of the deprivation of civil liberties.

Both men have not been charged and the authorities say that the case is under "summary pre-investigation." (Amnesty International Report, page 21; underlining supplied).

CHARLIE REVILLA PALMA, 25, a driver-electrician: He was arrested on December 12, 1974 in Cubao, Quezon City while entering a friend's house. He was, he said, "stabbed with a pistol in the stomach" and interrogated by six men who "took turns in boxing him in the stomach." When he fell from pain and exhaustion, they got him up, forced him against a wall, and "they mauled me again until I fell down." "Abalos came in with a *90v hand-cranked field telephone* and civilian informer Pat Ordona *attached one end of the wire to my thumb and the other end to my penis",* Palma told AI. *"Because of the pain, I shouted out loud until they stopped this kind of torture."*

The AI delegates said they saw scars from burns on Palma's left arm and also a ring of burns all around the lid of Palma's eyes. The AI Report quoted Palma as saying: "I was also offered a well-paying job and my release together with my wife by Major Joseph Patalinjug, if I would cooperate and *be a state witness against Father Edicio de la Torre. I refused his offer.*"

Palma's wife, Rosario, 21, was also arrested. She was released seven months later and placed "under house arrest." At the time of his arrest, Palma was a driver-electrician with Atlantic Gulf Corporation. (Amnesty International Report, p. 66; underlining supplied)

REYNALDO GUILLERMO, his wife ISABELITA: They were arrested on December 12, 1974, when they visited the apartment of their friends, Mr. and Mrs. Victor Quinto. He was, Reynaldo told AI, "beaten with a rifle while another man held my hands from behind" right there. The AI Report added: "They forced him to undress, tied up his hands and feet, and pushed him into a chair." Mrs. Guillermo confirmed this, testifying: "I was forced to watch my husband, wearing his briefs only, bound on the chair, beaten on his head, his chest, his arms, his shoulder blades, his stomach, with guns, long guns and pistols and fists."

Mrs. Guillermo was pregnant when she was arrested. According to Reynaldo's testimony, "they threatened to rape my wife and kill the fetus in her womb." Their child was born in detention. (Amnesty International Report, pp. 67-68).

JULIUS S. GIRON: Arrested on December 11, 1974, he was accused of being a ranking member of the Communist Party of the Philippines and a New People's Army (NPA) commander. He told AI: "My honest declaration of innocence was in vain. *Instead, by brutal force, I was made to accept self-incriminatory statements and declare FALSE TESTIMONIES* —Orlando Flores of NISA elbowed me on the sternum until I had difficulty breathing. This was followed by karate blows on the nape of my neck and strangulation of my esophagus by Lt. Arturo Lumibao of Zone-2. Lt. Garcia of M-2 struck me in the face several times. Lt. Cufford Cia of Zone-2 boxed me in the stomach. In my fear that I would come to the worst (death), I submitted myself to their desires, which was strongly against my will." (Amnesty International, pp. 70-71.)

WILFREDO R. HILAO, 30, a civil engineer, member of the Philippine Association of Civil Engineers: He was arrested on October 7, 1974, subjected to "Russian roulette." He was, he told AI, made to put a Magnum revolver against his head and made to pull the trigger "several times." He also recounted: "I was made to sit on a block of ice and when I was numb from cold, electric shock was applied from a hand-held dynamo. One terminal was wound directly to the end of my penis, another to a finger. The current was so strong I had to scream." (Amnesty International Report, p. 45.)

ROMEO TOLIO: Arrested on July 13, 1974, he was tortured shortly after his arrest. He claimed he was struck on the head with a lead pipe, and the AI delegates said "a scar was still visible" when they interviewed him. He also said electric shock was applied on his arms and the top of his head by officers he believed to be from METROCOM, Western Sector. He said he lost one tooth when a revolver was jammed into his mouth. He was, he told AI, *"coerced into signing a document."* (Amnesty International Report, p. 36).

For 13 days in the summer of 1975, June 22 to July 4, the AI Mission reported, a Lt. Aguinaldo "locked up ten women prisoners in a cramped room with only tin cans to hold urine ... One of the women was at least six months pregnant. All became sick to the extent that a doctor was called and all were treated for respiratory infection which subsequently spread to other prisoners of 5 CSU." (Amnesty International Report, p. 29)

It seems, despite Mr. Marcos' protestations to the civilized world that these were "aberrations," *the aberrations continue. Newsweek,* in its cover story, "The Push for Human Rights," reported:

> Officially, many repressive governments forbid torture. It has been outlawed in the Philippines, but security forces still maintain "safe houses" where they conduct torture (or 'tactical interrogations') at will. Maria Elena Ang, a 23-year-old student arrested last August, recalls *how a security agent brought in a hand-cranked electric generator and another made me drink glassfuls of water. Suddenly, the current shot painfully through my body. I could do nothing but scream and plead and then scream. (Newsweek,* June 20, 1977, p. 15; underlining supplied).

The most damning portion of the International Commission of Jurists report involved the prolonged detention and torture of martial law prisoners. The ICJ mission members conducted extensive interviews with detainees and visited various detention camps. Their report is fully documented, supported by affidavits. It shocks, when one reads it.

Any liberty-loving Filipino who reads the ICJ report should be shamed to the core of his being. Our foreign colonizers — Spaniards, Americans, Japanese — committed acts of barbarism on our people in the course of their occupations. But they were foreigners. Today, we are told, our Filipino brothers — in the employ of a domestic despot — have surpassed the foreigners in their inhumanity.

Part of the International Court of Justice report is as follows:

> Since the inception of Martial Law, the Government has arrested some 60,000 people. In May 1975 this number amounted to 50,551 persons, of whom 45,958 had at that time been released from custody, leaving 4,553 still under detention.
>
> In February 1977 precise figures were not available, but the Government stated that of the 60,000 persons arrested since the inception of Martial Law approximately 4,000 were still under detention. Of these, 1,400 were "subversive de-

tainees" and 2,500 were persons who allegedly had participated in the commission of a common crime. None of these had yet been brought to trial.

Of the 1,400 "subversive detainees," it can be reliably estimated that approximately 250 to 300 had been held for long periods of time, many as long as five years, or since the declaration of Martial Law in September 1972. The remaining 1,100 or so are a floating population which changes from time to time depending upon the incidence of arrests and release.

As already stated, in February 1977 we attended the habeas corpus hearings of ten detainees before the Supreme Court. Each had been held since the inception of Martial Law and had not at the time of the hearing been formally charged. No explanation for such an unreasonable period of detention was given by the Government. We visited several detention centers, namely Camp Bicutan, Camp Crame, the Youth Rehabilitation Center, and the Maximum Security Unit at Fort Bonifacio, as well as detention centers in Cebu, Davao City, and Tagum. We interviewed approximately 120 detainees as well as military officers responsible for their safety and well-being.

Our interviews led us to conclude that *the Government,* especially in cases involving alleged membership in or association with the Communist Party of the Philippines and/or the Moro National Liberation Front, *acts in an arbitrary and unreasonable way in that*

1. it fails to obtain the proper arrest warrants and arbitrarily picks up suspects, thereby denying them their legal safeguards;

2. detains these detainees without charges in private houses and places known as "safehouses";

3. regardless of the disciplinary proceedings mentioned later in this section, has condoned the infliction of torture by security agents of the military during sometimes very lengthy interrogation processes, using such methods as water treatment, electric shock, isolation for long periods of time chained to beds, etc., and physical beatings.

We found no instance of torture after the detainees had ultimately been turned over to a military camp or hospital. *The most shocking case was the death, as we believe while under interrogation by security agents, of a twenty-eight-year-old girl named Purificacion Pedro,* on which we will elaborate further in this report.

Perhaps the best way to document the aforesaid statements is to summarize very briefly the allegations made to us by 24 detainees, all of whom we found convincing. All these detainees had been arrested since January 1976:

Saturnino C. Ocampo, former assistant business editor and economic writer of the Manila Times; vice-president of the National Press Club of the Philippines 1970-71 and NPC director-secretary 1971-72; president of the Business-Economic Reporters' Association and director of his newspaper's workers' union. Arrested January 1976 and taken to operations center of the 1st Military Intelligence

Group (1MIG) at Camp Olivas, Pampanga, headquarters of the First Constabulary Zone; interrogated under duress by Major Benjamin Libarnes, executive officer of the First Police Constabulary Zone Intelligence Division, and officers of the 1MIG, Fifth Constabulary Security Unit (5CSU), Metrocom-Intelligence and National Intelligence and Security Authority (NISA). *Confined in solitary until taken on January 14 to a safehouse, manacled, blindfolded, subjected to electric shocks intensified by the pouring of cola drinks on his body, particularly at the points of electric contact; slapped on ears and nose, esophagus and head. Later burned on nipples and genitals; forced to eat excreta; threatened with castration and death.* Transferred to Fort Bonifacio, where he was interrogated by Col. Miguel Aure, Chief of 5CSU, and other officers of NISA and 5CSU. Subsequently abused by Lt. Rodolfo Aguinaldo of 5CSU and Lt. Antonio Baquiran of 1CSU. Kept in safehouse of 1CSU for seven weeks before being transferred to isolation cell at Camp Olivas. He was visited by First Police Constabulary Zone Commander Brig. Gen. Thomas P. Diaz, who did not believe Ocampo's torture reports until shown the marks on his body, then exclaimed "My God!" and promised that Ocampo would no longer be harmed. Ocampo was permitted visitors for one hour a week after two months of detention, and sunning and exercise after the third month. He was kept incommunicado from the other political prisoners. Transferred to Bicutan on July 6, 1976, but the next day was peremptorily taken away and placed in a solitary cell at the HPC Stockade in Camp Crame, where he was held incommunicado for three months, denied sunning, visitors and reading materials. Transferred to regular detention area for political detainees at HPC Stockade 4-B on October 1, 1976 — nearly nine months after his arrest.

Carlos Centenera was arrested January 11, 1976, by elements of the 5CSU; brought to a safehouse and *held incommunicado for five weeks, during which time he was beaten, strangulated with bare hands, electric wire, and steel bar such that his speech was impaired for two months; had bullets pressed between his fingers, hit with rifle butts and subjected twice to 'Russian roulette'; subjected to water cure for approximately thirty minutes and similarly to electric shocks.* Named Lt. Rodolfo Aguinaldo and Lt. Batac of 5CSU, Lt. Elnora Estrada of 5MIG (Intelligence Service, Armed Forces of the Philippines), and Lt. Alvarez of 5CSU as being present and participants in the torture sessions.

Guillermo Ponce de Leon was arrested on January 11, 1976, by elements of 5CSU; confined to a safehouse for ten days, where he was *stamped on, hogtied, and subjected to water cure, electric shock, and strangulation.* Named Capt. Milo Manlulu, Lt. Batac, Lt. Alvarez, and Sgt. Ricardo of the 5CSU, with Lt. Elnora Estrada of 5MIG (ISAFP) as his torturers.

Leonardo Manalo was arrested on January 11, 1976, by a joint team of 5CSU, 5MIG, NISA and Metrocom agents. Brought to two safehouses, where he was *beaten and kept incommunicado* for six days; *confined in a small toilet blindfolded and handcuffed for three days.* Kept incommunicado for a total of one and one-half months and contracted viral hepatitis.

Erlinda Tanve-Co was arrested January 14, 1976, at Olongapo City by elements of 1MIG (ISAFP), Z-2-1 CSU, with her five-year-old son; interviewed by Gen. Diaz and Col. Quila at Camp Olivas, and promised fair treatment. However, early the next morning she and her son were taken to a safehouse where she was separated from her son and incarcerated for twenty-five days, blindfolded and handcuffed to a metal bed, with intermittent torture by punching over the body, beating of the head, and sexual indignities. Was transferred to Female Detention Center on February 8, and her child permitted to join her. More than a year passed before she was given a formal charge sheet and informed that she would be arraigned on February 28, 1977. Her husband has been detained for seven years. She named Lt. Baquiren and Sgt. Lino Malabanan of 1MIG (ISAFP) as among her torturers.

Marcelino Tolam, Jr., y Magno was arrested on January 11, 1976 and taken to a safehouse where he saw two other detainees (Leonardo Manalo and Johnny Villegas) being tortured. In the presence of Col. Aure he was *beaten, punched, and kicked by about fourteen agents while seated with his arms tied behind the back of his chair, lighted cigarette butts pressed against his back and eyelids.* Those participating in the torture included Lt. Batac and Lt. Bibis. After transfer to a second safehouse, he was taken to CSU Camp Crame on January 13, where he was denied legal counsel, held incommunicado, and tortured by Lt. Amores. In the process of making statements without the benefit of legal counsel, he was *pistol-whipped.* Capt. Poblete participated in the physical intimidation of the witness at this stage.

Lualhati S. Roque, 25, was arrested on January 15, 1976, by First Police Constabulary Zone authorities. *Sexually abused and tortured* by Maj. Benjamin Libarnes, deputy and executive officer of the 1CSU 1 PC Zone, and Sgt. Lino Malabanan of 1MIG 1 PC Zone and others. Kept incommunicado for twenty-one days, and *denied rest or medical treatment despite weak heart* due to rheumatic condition.

Macario D. Tiu was arrested on February 4, 1976, by elements of the 4MIG, taken to Camp Evangelista, where he was tortured for two days, *beaten into unconsciousness* on the second night. After signing a statement without benefit of counsel, he was taken to Camp Alagar a week after his arrest.

Alfonso Abzagado was apprehended on July 21, 1976, by elements of the Criminal Investigation Service (CIS) without presentation of Arrest, Search and Seizure Order or warrant for arrest; taken to a safehouse and *subjected to water cure;* transferred to another safehouse of the 5CSU where he was *subjected to electric shocks, beating, cigarette burns, strangulation by rope.* Incarcerated for three weeks in a toilet until transferred to Camp Crame in isolation in mid August; thence Stockade 4 on October 16.

Ricardo Fajardo was also arrested on July 22, 1976, by elements of 5CSU and CIS; held in safehouse for three weeks and incommunicado for two months; *kicked and punched on various parts of his body.* Named Lt. Delfin and Lt. Aguinaldo of 5CSU as his tormentors.

Roberto Sunga was arrested on July 23, 1976, by 5CSU operatives; taken to safehouse, *beaten and pistol-whipped* and suffered permanent impairment of senses of smell and hearing; *subjected to electric shocks* and an attempt was made to compel him to subject a fellow detainee to the same treatment. Named Lt. Delfin and Lt. Rodolfo Aguinaldo of 5CSU and Capt. Saldajeno as being present and participating in the torture sessions.

Philip Limjoco y Espiritu was arrested on July 23, 1976, and *subjected to electric torture, cigarette and candle burns;* transferred to another safehouse after three or four days where he was *subjected to the water cure;* after three weeks in the safehouses he was transferred to 5CSU headquarters, where he was held incommunicado in isolation for five weeks. Only after three months was he transferred to the regular detention center at HPC Stockade 4-B.

Eugenio M. Magpantay was arrested by members of the 5CSU and 221st PC Company in Taytay on March 11, 1976. Was subjected by Sgt. Larry Untayas to *water cure, and was beaten* by the same officer. Transferred by 5CSU to safehouse on March 12, where he was *subjected to electric-shock torture.*

Joseph Gatus was arrested on August 1, 1976, by 5MIG (ISAFP) and taken to safehouse where he was *subjected to water cure, electric shock, cigarette burns, scalding, pistol-whipping, and beating;* held incommunicado for nineteen days and *urinated blood for several days as a consequence of these abuses.*

Meynardo G. Espeleta was arrested by elements of 5MIG (ISAFP) on August 4, 1976, held incommunicado for sixteen days, during which time he was *subjected to water cure and electric shock, slapped about the ears and face, strangulated, and a concentrated peppery substance placed on his lips and genitals.*

Maria Elena Ang was arrested on August 5, 1976, by a combined force of 5MIG (ISAFP/NISA) agents led by Maj. Uguerra; kept incommunicado for fifteen days at ISAFP headquarters in Bago-Bantay, Quezon City, and in a safehouse; *subjected to electric shock, water cure, sleep deprivation, sexual indignities, pistol-whipping, and threats to her relatives.* Named Maj. Uguerra and Maj. Liola of ISAFP, Atty. Castillo of NISA, and Lt. Batac of 5CSU as her torturers.

Jose Kitching was arrested on December 6, 1976; before he was taken to Bicutan seven weeks later on January 29, 1977, he had been *subjected to electric-shock treatment* at a safehouse and incommunicado; at the time of the interview, he had not undergone SPI (Special Preliminary Investigation).

Andrew Ocampo was arrested on October 17, 1976, apparently for being in possession of referendum literature, despite the decree ensuring freedom of discussion; he was *subjected to water cure and electric-shock treatment* at the M-2

Ninoy before Military Commission No. 2
on August 27, 1973.

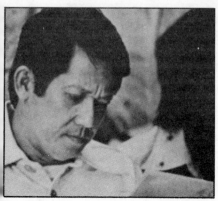

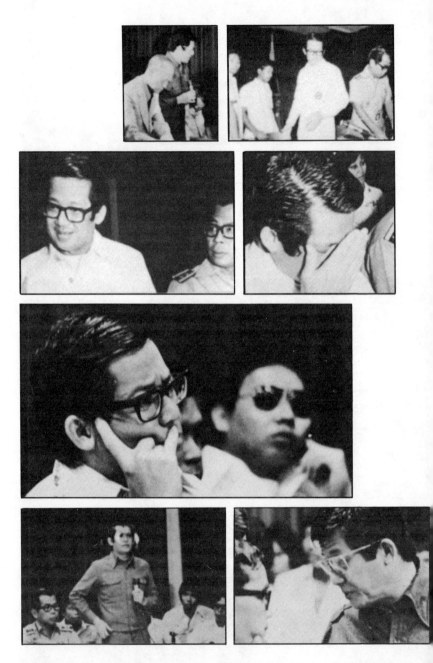

Proceedings in the Military Commission went on despite Ninoy's refusal to take part.

safehouse.

Willie Tatanis was arrested during the referendum period of October 1976 by agents of the M-2 and *subjected to electric shock and strangulation* and was kept incommunicado through one month in a safehouse codenamed the 'Shera Hotel'.

Juan Villegas was arrested in January 1976; taken to a safehouse where he was *beaten, strangulated, threatened with death, made to squat through one night,* and held incommunicado for a month before being taken to Camp Crame. At the time of the interview he had not been charged.

Mr. Nacariotu was arrested in Davao in February 1976; he was taken to a safehouse where he was *punched unconscious* and later taken to Camp Evangelista, where he underwent two SPI appearances but has not yet been charged.

William Postelion was arrested on January 11, 1976, and subjected to severe physical torture during eleven days in a safehouse before being transferred to Camp Crame. His SPI has proceeded, but he is not yet charged with offenses.

Juanito de los Reyes was arrested by Colonel Bibit on December 11, 1976; he was *beaten and kicked* during his initial interrogation and saw and heard the effects of torture on others; he *tried to commit suicide rather than undergo a similar ordeal,* but was prevented from doing so and transferred to Cebu after being held incommunicado for forty-three days by CSU.

Nathan Quimpo was arrested on October 9, 1976, by elements of the 7th RD, MSU, Philippine Army, at the Colegio de San Jose-Recoletos; taken handcuffed and blindfolded to Camp Lapu-Lapu, Cebu City. In the course of the tactical interrogation, *electric-shock treatment was applied, and he was punched and gun-whipped by a group of twelve men.* Presently detained in the Lahug Detention Center under austere conditions but permitted to engage in handicrafts and cook food brought in by visitors, who are restricted to their families and on religious.

Since we left the Philippines, we have been apprised of the following case:

Miss Trinidad Herrera, arrested on April 26, 1977. The details of this detention are not clear except that it appears that she was held incommunicado from April 26 to May 6, when she was located in a Manila detention center. Unconfirmed reports indicate that *she was given electric shocks* and her lawyer reports that "it took some time before she showed signs of recognizing me." It is reported that *"she would merely sit and stare blankly with tears rolling in her eyes."* She is president of Zoto, an organization of slum dwellers in Tondo which has questioned and opposed Mrs. Marcos' plans for slum clearance in this slum area in central Manila.

It is also reported that three other Zoto leaders have been arrested in an attempt to frustrate its annual meeting on May 15, 1977.

On the death of Purificacion Pedro ... There is strong circumstantial evidence that this young lady aged twenty-eight years was *killed by use of excessive force by overzealous security agents,* among whom are Colonel Miguel Aure and Lieutenant Garcia, who, with others operating out of the Fifth Constabulary Security Unit, have been repeatedly charged by victims of having inflicted torture from time to time during Martial Law.

The story of the death of Purificacion Pedro as stated below is based on interviews taken by us from the sister and brother of the victim, from close friends, and from the questioning by Mr. Butler and Professor Humphrey for over half an hour of the alleged perpetrator of the crime, Colonel Miguel Aure, at the offices of the Department of National Defense in Manila, in the presence of the Solicitor General, the Secretary of Defense, and other military officers.

Miss Pedro graduated tenth in the class of 1971 of the UP School of Social Work. She contemplated entering a religious order, but decided to work with the NASSA group on its Zone 1, Tondo program (in which Father de la Torre was active before his arrest in 1974).

On January 17, 1977, Miss Pedro told members of her family that she was going away for two or three days with friends; after her arrest she told her brother that those friends were associated with the New People's Army. They drove into the hills for several hours, and then walked through the night until about 7 a.m., when four others joined the group, all wearing sidearms. At about 10 a.m., the group was engaged in a clash with a patrol of the Philippine Constabulary; Miss Pedro was shot in the shoulder and captured, while her associates escaped.

Miss Pedro was taken to Bataan Provincial Hospital and operated on for her wounds, which were not critical. She was placed under heavy guard in the hospital's X-ray room. When her family visited her in the hospital, she expressed real apprehension about her safety and said that she had been interrogated already by seven teams, including Colonel Aure of the CSU. Despite his skepticism, her brother arranged for his sisters to stay by her room throughout the next days. According to the affidavit of Mrs. Carmen P. Gaspar, sister of the detainee, four men in civilian clothes ordered her out of Miss Pedro's room at about 5:45 p.m. on January 23, 1977. She identified one of the men as Lieutenant Garcia. It was Lt. Garcia who, when he emerged from the room at about 6:15 p.m., informed Mrs. Gaspar that her sister was incommunicado. At about 6:30 p.m., the evening meal for Miss Pedro was delivered to the inside guard; a few minutes later the inside guard called to the outside guard. Mrs. Gaspar caught the word "Bigti" ("Hang") and rushed in. She was the first to enter the bathroom.

"We found my sister in a standing position, her upper body leaning toward the corner, with a cord tied to her neck. I supported her head up to help her breathe (I was hoping she was still alive), and I felt her dress was wet, all the while that I was waiting for the guard to get a knife.

"Both feet were on the floor, with her head leaning towards the corner near the towel rack. She was not facing away from the wall. (When I heard the guard say the word 'Bigti' before I saw her, I had imagined that I would find her tongue sticking out, and with her feet some distance from the floor. But it was not so.)

"As I clasped her body, I noticed that her clothes were wet, but the floor was dry, as I was barefoot. (I had left my step-ins in the corridor).

"The towel rack to which the hanging cord was tied was only five feet five inches from the ground. My sister is about five feet. Someone then cut the hanging cord first, and then the cord tied to her neck, and they carried her (by that time a number of people were on hand to help) to another wing of the hospital. I followed them inside the emergency room but someone led me out. I waited outside crying. About fifteen to twenty minutes later, when the door opened, I knew from their face that my sister was dead. They brought her back to her room. At around 7:15 p.m. or thereabouts the doctor came to examine her and confirmed her dead. As I was wiping her body after the doctors had pronounced her dead, I found a medal clenched in her right hand. It was the Miraculous Medal which my sister Aurora had given the day before she died."

No autopsy was performed on Miss Pedro's body. The death certificate issued by Dr. Ernesto S. Soriano indicated that the victim died of asphyxiation due to strangulation by hanging. According to an investigation conducted by two separate agencies of the Bataan Constabulary Judge Advocate, it was asserted that while Col. Miguel Aure had visited her on the forenoon of her death, "it was established that Col. Aure and his men had already left the hospital when Purificacion Pedro asked permission to go inside the toilet where she was later found dead." This investigation placed Col. Aure's arrival at the hospital at "about 4:30 o'clock in the afternoon." The statements of the inside guards placed the arrival of the interrogation team between 4:30 and 5:00 p.m. and stated that they were in the room for some forty-five minutes. The military authorities hold that Miss Pedro's death was a suicide.

We have serious reservations concerning the accuracy of the government's finding arising from the following observations:

1. There was no autopsy ordered.

2. A review of her past life and nature leads us to believe that she was not suicidal.

3. There were indications that she died from drowning rather than from asphyxiation by hanging.

4. Our questioning of the military security agents involved produced, in our opinion, serious questions concerning their credibility.

5. The fact that death occurred within an hour of the admitted interrogation of Miss Pedro.

We are citing this case not to imply that these security agents were acting on direct instructions of the Government (although we hope that their involvement will be thoroughly investigated), but to illustrate the use of excessive force inherent in any martial law or military regime. (ICJ Report, pp. 30-36; underlining supplied)

If these cases of man's inhumanity to man revulse the sensibilities of civilized men, they are nothing compared to the thoroughly dehumanizing, indescribable sufferings reserved by the Marcos martial law Gestapo for Mr. Marcos' political enemies, actual and fancied. They are only now coming to light, but already they tell a tale of premeditated violence, torture and dehumanization to break the human spirit, reduce men into whimpering animals, make them testify against themselves and their fellowmen.

Here are only a few such cases, all completely documented and sworn to by the victims:

ALEXANDER C. AREVALO, 22, a casino employee: He was arrested on September 24, 1972 without any Warrant of Arrest served on him, was implicated in the alleged plot to assassinate Mr. Marcos only when lawyers appeared for him before the Supreme Court, pleading for his right to the Writ of Habeas Corpus, on February 1, 1977. His story: When he was arrested, his "arms were tied with a gun belt"; when he was brought to Fort Bonifacio, "they changed the belt with a manacle"; *for one month, he was kept in the Photo Lab of M.S.U. (Maximum Security Unit), "without my handcuffs being removed even if I ate, bathed, moved my bowels, or slept";* then he was transferred to MS.U. 1571, where he was *kept in solitary confinement for nine months and "for three weeks I had to feel with my hands and smell the food that was provided: I ate them without knowing what they were, because there were no lights."* He was beaten and subjected to electric shocks while manacled and blindfolded in his initial interrogations; he knelt on his knees and "pleaded for mercy," because his liver and kidney had been only recently operated on, "but they ignored my pleas and continued beating me." He was allowed no visitors, prohibited from talking to anyone; when his plea to be permitted visits by his family was refused, he threatened and actually attempted suicide. He was finally allowed his first visitors on his ninth month. He is still in M.S.U. 1571.

MANUEL F. DAEZ, 42, a father of four, caretaker of ex-Sen. Sergio Osmena, Jr.: Arrested on October 9, 1972, he has not been tortured. But his is a pathetic plaint: "On the second night, I was again transferred to another place blindfolded with both hands handcuffed. I stayed in this place for months before I was allowed to be visited. *I have been crying almost every day because of surprise for the situation I am now in and also because this is the first time I have been detained.* Here, light and water was rationed only by schedule. *Food was given to me, like a dog, shoved under the iron grills.* I was in solitary for two months." Like Arevalo, he was arrested without warrant, was not charged for five (5) years until lawyers petitioned the Supreme Court for his right to the Writ, and remains in M.S.U. 1571.

MARCELO FERRER, 58, a father of five, a driver: Arrested on September 26, 1972, he has not been physically beaten. He was, he said, asked about the movements of his amo, the failed Manila Mayoralty candidate of Mr. Marcos' own Nacionalista Party in 1971, Mr. Eduardo Figueras, and he "fortrightly answered all the questions." He said he could not say why Figueras went to certain places because: "A driver just follows where his master tells him to go. A driver does not ask his master why he is going to such and such a place. He just drives to where he is directed to go." He was placed in solitary confinement for four months in a prison cell 4-1/2 feet in width, 11-1/2 feet in length, with steel bars and 3-1/2 feet away, there is a wooden door with a 5" x 7" small window." In his confinement, he got sick of advanced TB, which compelled his M.S.U. jailors to move him to the Station Hospital. He is back in "my old cell," charged with complicity in the claimed plot to kill Mr. Marcos only when he, with Arevalo, Daez, and seven others, were represented by lawyers in the Supreme Court on February 1, 1977 almost five years after his arrest.

MARCELO GALLARIN, 50, a rubber stamp maker and Figueras leader: He was seized on October 28, 1972, given fist blows, subjected to electric shock, detained in a small, poorly ventilated cell, fed "like a dog or a cat" while he was kept in solitary confinement for four months. *"I was manacled behind my back* for four continuous days and three nights," he tells in his sworn statement. *"So that when I went to the toilet to do my toilet or urine, they did not remove the manacles or even put it in front.* It was always placed behind my back and I had to position myself by sitting on a chair and resting my chin on the desk. Even while sleeping that I hardly had any sleep. *It is hard to sleep with your hands manacled behind your back."* He, too, remains in M.S.U. 1571.

ROMUALDO INDUCTIVO, a father of seven, a driver of Figueras: He was arrested on September 26, 1972, initially brought to Malacañang, moved to Fort Bonifacio and, on November 1, 1972, was brought back to Malacañang, where he was *kept in handcuffs for a week,* subjected to slappings and electric shocks. "When I could no longer stand the pain of the electric shocks, I begged them and I said I am already old — for them not to treat me like that," his Sworn Statement narrates. *"They did not remove the handcuffs even while I ate, moved my bowel, took a bath."* He was returned to Fort Bonifacio on November 7, where, as he tells: "I was in *solitary confinement for six (6) months.* Talking with anybody was prohibited; they get angry. *My food was being given by passing it under the bars. And if the food was thrown, it gets spilled in the cement floor."* His case status: the same as the others.

FAUSTINO SAMONTE, 43, father of six, a messenger of Figueras: He was taken on December 18, 1972, initially lodged in the Malabon municipal jail, then transferred to Malacañang Park and kept in solitary confinement for four months in an unlighted cell, where: *"The food was passed to me under the door as if I were an animal. And when the food ration came after night had fallen, I would just smell and feel by touch the food I was eating.* I was forbidden to speak to anyone. I was in complete solitary. I was also forbidden to look out the window." His interrogators wanted him to tell about shipments of chemicals withdrawn for Figueras from customs, but he didn't know "the left and right of the procedure in withdrawing shipments"; each time he angered his inquisitors, they beat him up; one time so badly that he *"almost lost consciousness."* He was allowed visits by his family only seven months after — "and, even then, only my wife and children could visit me." His mother was 73 years old, with heart trouble, but his jailors didn't consider her as "family"; he had to make a special request for her visit. His status: Ditto.

RODOLFO MACASALABANG, 44, unemployed. Arrested on September 27, 1972, he was manacled, taken from one place to another blindfolded, severely beaten and tortured with electric shocks in each place. For almost one month, he tells, *"I ate with my hands manacled, I moved my bowels with my hands manacled that I could clean myself only with tremendous difficulty. It was never removed even when I slept, so that I had great difficulty in sleeping.* Sometimes when they allowed me to take a bath, they removed it." He, too, is now implicated in the so-called assassination plot — more than five years after his arrest without Warrant, without charges. (Underlining supplied)

There are ten of them in all, small people who, by no stretch of the imagination, could be regarded as conspirators, let alone the brains, in any plot to assassinate and stage a coup d'etat against the all-powerful Mr. Marcos. But, as one of their jailors was candid enough to tell them, in Arevalo's telling, "there was no case against us" and they would be freed once Serging Osmeña came home. As another M.S.U. jailor, with equal candor, told them, "It is Senator Osmeña we want, not you small people."

Two others — Policarpio A. Rosales, 50, a father of six, operator of a small camera repair shop in Quiapo, and Juanito Samson, 43, a small trader and father of seven — have been under M.S.U. detention since September 18, 1974. They are being forced, Rosales' affidavit tells, to say Vice-President Lopez gave them P3.5 million, in two suitcases, to assassinate Mr. Marcos. "To this I could never agree," he says, "because it is not true...Mr. Lopez does not even know me."

Parenthetically, how Rosales' interrogation went is revelatory. In his affidavit, he relates:

After a month, we were again investigated by Col. Antonio P. Uy and his companions whose identities I cannot remember. During the investigation, whenever the questions would touch on the issue of the financier and the bringing of the money to the hotel and I would answer them, the one typing will immediately butt in and say, "Sir, there is a complication," and the other will order, "Change it, reform it," The questions are repeatedly asked.

After we were through and they asked me to sign, and I read it, I noticed that *there were statements I said which were deleted and there were statements that I did not say but were added and other answers were changed completely.* When I told them it was not what I said, they said it was just the same and it would be better for me just to admit my guilt and the President may even forgive me. My tormentors said, "You just sign so you can go home." It was already past midnight that we finished, about 1:00 o'clock when I was brought back to my cell with my eyes blindfolded. (Underlining supplied)

For this and similar other jobs, I imagine, Colonel Uy has been rewarded with a star. He is now Brig. Gen. Antonio P. Uy.

What happened to Rosales is very tragic. On July 3, 1977, he died while still under detention — not formally accused before any court, civil or military, but held prisoner nevertheless for reasons of national security and for possible prosecution."

In the plaintive words of his counsel: "Is death the only way petitioners could regain their freedom?"

It has become quite obvious, as former Senator Lorenzo M. Tañada, former Senator Jose W. Diokno and Attorney Joker Arroyo, counsel for the M.S.U. Ten, have said: "they (the Ten) have been arrested, tortured and detained indefinitely to extract evidence from them against themselves or other persons." Mr. Marcos needed political show trials to back up the claim he made when he instituted martial law — that a rightist-communist conspiracy was in operation, that the Republic was imperilled — and his dutiful Brown Shirts sought to provide him with evidence, witnesses and testimonies required by these so-called trials under his dictatorship.

If these are not Star Chamber methods, then what are they? If this is not Marcos-style Inquisition, what is it? If this is not torturing evidence into existence, what do we call it?

The facts stand out. They are incontrovertible.

And the very same brutalities, cruelties and indignities — tortures! — have been visited by Mr. Marcos' Brown Shirts upon our people in the effort to stage my own show trial. Their families have had to suffer the same painful experiences.

Many of the civilian witnesses presented by the prosecution to testify against me have been detained for periods ranging from a week to six months.

The reports I have received tell me that these detentions, whether lasting a week or some months, have all involved trips into the chambers of Mr. Marcos' Inquisition.

Their wives went to my wife for guidance. When my wife reported to me the sad predicament of these friends and former co-workers, I told her to tell them to sign any affidavit against me — if this would restore their freedom. I held: This martial law regime may have already destroyed me beyond salvation; there is no reason why others must be made to share my fate.

I have quoted extensively from the reports of Amnesty International, recipient of the Nobel Peace Prize, and the International Commission of Jurists. I have done so as I find their relations truly shocking and unforgettable after having been held incommunicado for the last five years. In fact, it was only after my "visit" to Mr. Marcos in Malacañang last June 1977 that I was allowed to read newspapers and other publications.

The reports of the two prestigious international organizations should meet every test of objectivity and credibility. Both are singularly committed to fostering humanity and morality in the world's governments. In fact, Amnesty International was awarded the most coveted prize given by civilized society — the Nobel Peace Prize — for painstakingly documenting human-rights violations in many countries and unflaggingly asking for an end to them.

The mission members had no personal friends among the detainees. In fact, many of them were visiting the Philippines for the first time. They had no ax to grind, no biases whatsoever, in their work to uncover the ugly truths of Mr. Marcos' martial rule.

The missioners interviewed jailed and jailors — detainees and government officials. They attended hearings in the Supreme Court and the military tribunals. They met with leading elements of the religious, the academe and the law profession, and other concerned citizens — as well as with the leading administrators of martial law.

Both organizations expressed opposition to the trial of civilians by military tribunals even during a state of emergency. They found particularly objectionable the provision of Presidential Decree No. 39 which placed civilians under the jurisdiction of military tribunals and, what was more odious, denied the accused their right to counsel.

The Integrated Bar of the Philippines has objected to these procedures, as well as others, on the ground that they unduly enlarge the intervention of the armed forces in civilian matters and seriously and severely undermine the role of the civilian judicial process. According to the ICJ investigators, some members of the IBP informed them that military authorities had on several occasions "even threatened to detain defense lawyers who came to the assistance of their clients."

In the view of the ICJ missioners, the civil courts of the Philippines, with their civilian judges and prosecutors, are more than adequate to perform the judicial functions and to administer the process of law under martial law. In their considered view: "Military tribunals are unnecessary and unwarranted."

I must say, at this point, that I welcome these and other developments in the field of human rights. I am particularly heartened by — and take to heart — President Carter's inaugural commitment:

> The passion for freedom is on the rise. Tapping this new spirit, there can be no nobler nor more ambitious task for America to undertake on this day of a new beginning than *to help shape a just and peaceful world that is truly humane... Because we are free, we can never be indifferent to the fate of freedom elsewhere.* Our moral sense dictates a clearcut preference for those societies which share with us an abiding respect for individual human rights. We do not seek to intimidate, but it is clear that *a world which others can dominate with impunity would be inhospitable to decency and a threat to the well-being of all peoples. . . . Our commitment to human rights must be absolute.* (Underlining supplied)

It is not only a breath of fresh air, but the burst of a new spring. What a welcome change it is from the *realpolitik* of prior U.S. policy!

I welcome, as well, Mr. Marcos' own public commitments, late in the day though it be for the likes of Charlie Palma, Maria Elena Ang, Alexander Arevalo and Trining Herrera. He said, of Trining's case: "No single case of maltreatment is to me permissible. One solitary victim is enough to arouse my anger."

It may be too late for us, but it may spare those who are yet untouched but who, if this rule of injustice, brutality and falsehood continues unabated, may yet find themselves on the martial law rack. To help give substance to Mr. Marcos' word, may I commend to him the counsel of the late Pope Pius XII.

> The function of law, its dignity and the concept of natural equity for man requires punitive action ... based .. not upon arbitrariness and passion but upon clear and firm judicial procedure. This requires that there be at the very least judicial action, must not follow caprice but must respect judicial procedure. *It is not permissible that a man without guilt be arbitrarily arrested and simply disappear into prison. It is a mockery of justice to send someone to a concentration camp and hold him there without normal legal process.* (Extract from the message of His Holiness Pope Pius XII, 6th International Congress of Penal Law, Rome, September 26, 1953; underlining supplied)

IX

RA 1700—THE ANTI-SUBVERSION ACT

> We cannot overemphasize the need for
> prudence and circumspection in the en-
> forcement of the Anti-Subversion Act,
> operating as it does in the sensitive areas
> of freedom of expression and belief.
>
> —PEOPLE V. FERRER,
> 48 SCRA, DEC. 27, 1972

T HE MAJOR charges against me turn on alleged violations of Republic Act No. 1700, the Anti-Subversion Law. There are four separate charges; a total of nine specifications.

In the face of all these charges I say: I am not guilty!

RA 1700 was enacted by Congress in the hysterical mid-fifties when "communism" was synonymous with the Soviet bloc — a worldwide empire of 81 communist parties "controlled, directed and financed" by the Kremlin. Communism meant "systemic war" — wars by proxy waged by Soviet Russia in Asia, the Middle East and Latin America, though not yet in Black Africa. The communist scoreboard boasted of these major gains in the decade or two after the end of World War II:

- In Eastern Europe, Soviet hegemony established as far as Soviet tanks and troops had reached at the end of World War II, was completed when Czech communists threw out the last non-communists in the Czech government in 1948.

- In Asia, Mao Tse-tung had driven Chiang Kai-shek to Taiwan in 1949. North Korea had invaded South Korea in 1950 bringing about the first battle between Free World and communist forces in a war that came to a stalemated truce in 1953, and Ho Chi Minh had defeated France in Dien Bien Phu in 1954, partitioning Vietnam into a communist North and a "free" South and, in the view of many then, exposing not only the rest of Indochina, but all of Southeast Asia, to the communist tide.

- In Latin America, Col. Jacobo Arbenz, a communist, had taken power in 1951, which encouraged "fraternal" stirrings all over Central and South America, areas the U.S. had forbidden to any designing outside forces under the Monroe doctrine.

- In the Middle East, by the mid-fifties, Syria had turned very pro-Soviet, Egypt was armed and financed by the Soviet Union sufficiently for Nasser to seize the Suez Canal in 1956 and touch off a communist uprising in Jordan in 1957. In the Jordanian affair, Syria, Egypt and the Palestinians were joined by the Kremlin in openly encouraging the rebels fighting King Hussein's Jordanian Legion; Moscow backed down only upon the entry of the U.S. Sixth Fleet on the scene, thereby quelling the rebellion.

It was against this Soviet "systemic war" backdrop that SEATO and other Free World military alliances were forged by John Foster Dulles, President Eisenhower's Secretary of State, who formulated the "Domino Theory" to "contain" the cresting communist tidal wave. The Philippines, in the Manila Conference of 1954, was a signatory of the Southeast Asia Treaty Organization, which completed the Free World's chain of defense around the communist lands — starting with NATO in Europe, CENTO in the Middle East, SEATO in Southeast Asia, and ending with the network of U.S. bilateral arrangements with Japan, Taiwan and South Korea in Northeast Asia.

Anti-communist analysts were quick to point to, in the words of one document, "the essential sameness and continuity of communist techniques, attitudes and strategic approach." *Vide,* they said, how Soviet Russia seized China through Mao, took North Vietnam through Ho, almost overran South Korea through Kim II Sung and Laos through Souvanna Phouma. The Huk rebellion crushed by Magsaysay in the Philippines, the Malayan communist insurgency being fought by General Templer in Malaya, and the Partai Kommunis Indonesia movement in Indonesia, they held, were marked by an "essential sameness."

Communism was "a monolith," with the Soviet Union as the pith of the Communist Empire and all the other communist countries, including People's China satellites, operated in a larger domain ruled or dominated by the men in the Kremlin. Communist China's leaders were Moscow-trained and, therefore, Moscow-influenced, if not Moscow-directed — so went the prevailing geopolitical gospel.

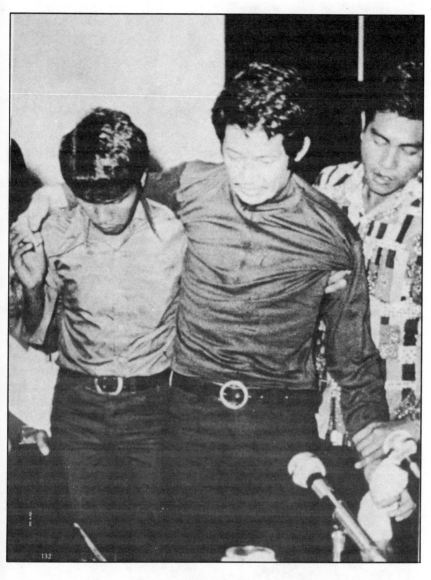

Ninoy is brought by soldiers to Military Commission hearing while still on hunger strike.

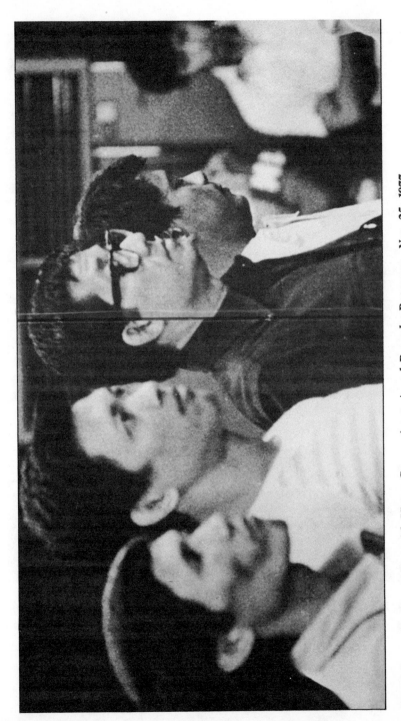

Ninoy hears death sentence with Victor Corpus (center) and Bernabe Buscayno, Nov. 25, 1977.

Internally, in many countries, the panicky outlook — a murky world of world-wide communist conspiracy! — bred witch-hunters, Red-catchers and Ku Klux-ers, super-zealots who vilified, crucified and destroyed any one whom they suspected of being communist, pinko or fellow-traveler. In the United States, the great American nightmare, McCarthyism, was born. In the Philippines, it found an echo in the infamous CAFA (Committee on Anti-Filipino Activities) Inquisition.

This was in the mid-fifties. Dien Bien Phu had fallen, the British under General Templer were being harassed by the communist insurgents in Malaya, the Burmese Red and White Flag communists were knocking at the very gates of Rangoon, and the Huk, despite the roundup of the CPP politburo by Magsaysay, were held to have merely taken the Leninist "one step backward" tactic. Any support for communism was tantamount to treason — and the professional patriots saw Reds, Pinks and villains of other hues hiding in many a closet, patiently awaiting their "next moment" to do "Moscow's bidding."

The world was divided ideologically into a Free World and a Sino-Soviet Bloc with Peking, as perceived, no less a Soviet fief than the lesser communist satellites. The neutralists, like India, were fence-sitters; they were yet far from being accepted as part of the Third World, the non-aligned.

It was strictly in keeping with the hysteria of the time that Congress passed RA 1700. A new law had to be enacted, because the provision of the Penal Code covering rebellion did not envision the new element of "an alien power taking over control and domination of the Republic."

It was the fear of an "alien power's domination" that gave rise to RA 1700. And the new word "subversion" found its way into our statute books. To overthrow a government by force and violence is rebellion. But to overthrow it, establish a totalitarian form of government, and place it under the control and domination of an alien power is "subversion."

However, by the late sixties and early seventies, barely 25 years after the end of World War II, communism, the dreaded ideology, had acquired new meanings, new interpretations, new centers. Today, we have Soviet communism — the original — being challenged by Chinese communism, Yugoslav communism, Euro-communism, the communism of Latin America and the communism of the Arab states. Even small nations like Albania have come up with their own mutations.

That communism has multiple facets is now an accepted fact and the world is now witness to a new communist phenomenon — that whenever a communist peo-ple wins political power and gives birth to a new communist state, it splits from the main body of the Soviet type and comes up with its own interpretation. Unless, of course, it is directly under the sway of Soviet military might, as in the case of East Germany.

Like Christianity, new sects have developed from the main corpus, giving rise to various interpretations of the "truth" and the "correct way" of development. As Arrigo Levi, editor-in-chief of Italy's leading newspaper *La Stampa,* recently noted: "As a result of an accumulation of splits and heresies, communism as a universal ideology is dead."

Levi, an astute observer of Euro-communism and who has faithfully chronicled the rise and growth of Italy's Communist Party, described the phenomenon thus:

> Communism as a church is a memory from the past; it is more habit than faith. Foreign communists may still "go to Moscow," as some people go to Mass on Sunday, in spite of being total miscreants. Nonetheless, it seems possible that the "splitting" phenomenon has now reached, through accumulation, the stage of a quantum leap, where everything becomes totally different.

The original beliefs ingrained in a world-wide communist movement are not only being discarded but are, in the words of one observer, "in disrepute" — including the myth of the October Revolution. Soviet Russia, the great experiment and model, has failed to live up to its billings. Such is its technological backwardness that it is now exerting frantic efforts to attract Western technological knowhow. Its unprecedented massive imports of agricultural products from the "imperialist" states, like the United States, starkly reflect its economic difficulties. "Shocking," said a developing country leader, who in earlier days would have been a Soviet *ad hoc* proxy, "are (the Soviets') lack of modernity in all respects, including matters of cultural and political liberties."

The Soviet Empire, the communist monolith, is not only fissured, it is fragmented — as revealed by Yugoslavia's Tito, Spain's Carillo and Italy's Berenguer to Soviet Party boss Leonid Brezhnev's face during the latest summit of the Communist International. Rightly, as one watcher of the scene noted, "communism is fighting a rear-guard action against the haunting ghost of democracy."

Such changes — the Sino-Soviet split, the many mutations in the communist camp — have not been lost to us. As early as 1969, we, the Filipino leadership, Nacionalistas and Liberals alike, came to the singular conclusion: the spectre we feared was gone; it was time to repeal RA 1700. It had, we held, "outlived its usefulness."

Legal experts questioned RA 1700's constitutionality, something nobody dared do in the hysteria of the fifties. RA 1700, these experts said, was a bill of attainder. It embraced more than one subject not expressed in the title; it was vague and, worse, it denied the equal protection of the laws.

In fact, Rep. Joaquin R. Roces (N, Manila), who, as a chairman of the Committee of Anti-Filipino Activities, authored RA 1700 in 1957, led the bipartisan movement for repeal.

In fact, too, Mr. Marcos joined in the advocacy for repeal — in his presidential reelection campaign of 1969. RA 1700, Mr. Marcos correctly observed, was a stumbling block to normalization by the Philippines of diplomatic relations with the socialist or communist countries.

In 1970-71, the move to repeal RA 1700 was formalized. A repeal bill was filed by a vast majority of the senators — some 15 of us, if I recall rightly; a bipartisan group, Nacionalistas and Liberals.

The first real, legal test of RA 1700 came on March 5, 1970. A criminal complaint for violation of RA 1700 was filed against Leoncio Co in the Tarlac Court of First Instance. On March 10, 1970, Judge de Guzman of the Tarlac CFI conducted a preliminary investigation. He found a *prima facie* case against Co. He directed the government prosecutors to file the corresponding information.

Meanwhile, on May 25, 1970, another criminal complaint was filed against Nilo Tayag and five others for violation of the same act, RA 1700, also in the Tarlac CFI. After a preliminary investigation, the corresponding information was filed against Tayag et al.

On July 21, 1970, Tayag's counsel moved to quash. They argued on these grounds: 1) It is a bill of attainder; 2) it is vague; 3) it embraces more than one subject not expressed in the title; 4) it denies the equal protection of the laws.

On September 15, 1970, Judge Simeon Ferrer of the Tarlac CFI declared the statute void and unconstitutional. The government appealed to the Supreme Court.

On December 27, 1972, three months after the declaration of martial law, the Supreme Court ruled — in People vs. Ferrer, 48, SCRA, Dec.27, 1972 — that RA 1700 is valid and constitutional. However, the Supreme Court laid down "basic guidelines" in any prosecution under RA 1700:

In addition to proving such circumstances as may effect liability, the government must establish the following elements of the crime of joining the Communist Party of the Philippines or any other subversive organization:

(1) In the case of subversive organizations other than the Communist Party of the Philippines: (a) that the purpose of the organization is to overthrow the present government of the Philippines and to establish in this country a totalitarian regime *under the domination of a foreign power;* (b) that the accused *joined* such organization; and (c) that he did so willingly, knowingly and by overt acts; and

(2) In the case of the Communist Party of the Philippines: (a) that the CPP continues to pursue the objectives which led Congress in 1957 to declare it to be an organized conspiracy for the overthrow of the Government by illegal means for the purpose of placing the country *under the control of a foreign power;* (b) that the accused *joined* the CPP; and (c) that he did so willfully, knowingly and by overt acts. (Underscoring supplied)

The decision was penned by then Justice Fred Ruiz Castro, former AFP judge advocate general. It was concurred in by Justices Makalintal, Zaldivar, Teehankee, Barredo, Esguerra, Makasiar, Antonio and Concepcion. Justice Fernando dissented.

On August 3, 1976, before I was arraigned, I moved to quash the subversion charges against me because the charge sheet failed to specify a *vital element* of the charge. For the charge to be valid, I pointed out, the prosecution must specify that one of my aims is to place this country "under the domination" and "under the control of a foreign power."

To be able to defend myself adequately, I must know *which is this alien power.*

In my motion to quash, I asked the trial counsel to specify the "foreign power." He refused, saying that my arraignment was not the time or the place for that. But he promised to reveal this mysterious alien power "in the course of the proceedings."

Under RA 1700, the alien power clearly referred to by Congress was a communist power. It meant the USSR. Later, it included the People's Republic of China, because the NPAs were often referred to as "Maoist NPAs" by government authorities.

I cannot understand the hesitancy of the trial counsel to identify the "alien power." Why?

The law member peremptorily denied my motion to quash. The least I expected from him was to ask the trial counsel to specify the "foreign power" even if he denied my motion to quash.

As I argued before this Commission, it is not enough, for example, that I be charged with murder. The man I was supposed to have murdered must be specified — and also the time and the place of the crime. By the same token, it is not enough that I be charged with seeking to place this country under the domination and control of an alien power. The alien power must be specified at the time of my arraignment, so I can enter a correct plea.

To specify the "foreign power" after my arraignment is most anomalous. It is tantamount to pleading under an incomplete charge!

A careful reading of Proclamation 1081 would eliminate the Soviet Union and would clearly identify the People's Republic of China as the "foreign power" that allegedly gave "active" and "material support" to the domestic communist dissidents, the "Maoist NPAs."

The first "Whereas" of 1081 identifies only "a foreign power" (most definitely in the singular!) whose "political, social, economic, legal and moral precepts are based on Marxist-Leninist-Maoist teachings and beliefs."

The Soviet Union adheres to the Marxist-Leninist teachings and beliefs, but definitely not to the Maoist variant. The only major power that follows the Marxist-Leninist-Maoist teachings and beliefs is the People's Republic of China.

Proclamation 1081 was signed on September 21, 1972.

The Supreme Court's basic guidelines that must be followed in any prosecution under RA 1700 appeared in the decision of People vs. Ferrer, 48 SCRA, December 27, 1972.

I was first informed of the charges against me on August, 1973. (Up to this date, the Philippines had no diplomatic relations with the People's Republic of China.)

On September 20, 1974, almost two years to the day Mr. Marcos declared martial rule and tagged the People's Republic of China as the main supporter of the CPP/NPA, he dispatched his wife Imelda on an "historic and unprecedented" 10-day visit to Peking to "seek an understanding with the Chinese leaders on possible and desirable areas of increased cooperation between the two countries."

Mrs. Marcos met with Premier Chou En-lai and was granted an "audience" with the Great Helmsman himself, Chairman Mao Tse-tung. The television crew caught Mrs. Marcos giving the Chairman's sagging pink cheeks a reverent kiss. In her awe and excitement, Mrs. Marcos was moved to tears. The TV eye caught all this for posterity.

Mrs. Marcos made a pilgrimage to the caves of Yenan, the shrine of the Chinese communist revolution. This, too, was dutifully recorded — and televised back home.

In her report upon her return to the Foreign Policy Council, Mrs. Marcos was quoted by the Malacañang Press Office as saying:

> I came to China with an open mind. China's political leaders — from Chairman Mao to the ranking officials of provincial and municipal revolutionary councils — all expressed a sincere desire to be friends. *I did not believe that the Chinese ever entertained the belief that we could ever be persuaded to abandon our political system.* (Underscoring mine)

Two years after her husband tagged the People's Republic of China as the evil foreign power that subverted and attempted to overthrow our government with arms, logistics and other kinds of aid to the local CPP/NPA, Mrs. Marcos debunked the claim as a fervent pilgrim to Peking.

If we are to believe Mrs. Marcos, the Chinese never believed they could ever persuade the Filipinos to abandon their political system. Therefore, there is no logic or truth in the claim that they attempted to overthrow our existing political system and replace it with their own by using the local CPP/NPAs as proxies — since, in Mrs. Marcos' happy report, they believed it was doomed from the beginning.

Mrs. Marcos has been so captivated by Communist China's great leap forward that as late as early this month (December 1977), in an interview with syndicated American columnist William Buckley, she was still gushing and heaping praise on Chairman Mao. She was, she said in sum, the Chairman's fervent devotee — and the paeans she sang, in the greatest superlatives and the most lyrical terms, affirmed what she said she was, a confirmed convert to the Way of Mao.

Buckley wanted to know why the Marcoses, as reported by *Time* magazine, admired Mao the most among the world's contemporary figures. To admire Mao for effecting a certain ideological unity in his people, according to Buckley, is on the order of admiring Adolf Hitler for effecting a certain ethnic unity among the Germans. He saw, one could see, a particular strain of radical intensity in Imelda's idolatrous adulation for the recently departed Communist Chinese Helmsman.

In his interview with the voluble Imelda, Buckley found the answer. Imelda told him:

> *I have known three Popes...I tell you there is nobody who radiates the kind of holiness that flowed out of Chairman Mao.*

Puzzled after his encounter with Imelda, Buckley asked: "What is a woman like Imelda doing, worshipping at the altar of Mao Tse-tung?" What Buckley did not know was that while Imelda was worshipping at the altar of Mao, hundreds of idealistic young Filipinos were languishing in the Marcoses' cruel martial law prisons for having read and followed so-called Mao Tse-tung Thought.

From June 7 to 11, 1975, Mr. Marcos made his own personal pilgrimage to Peking and there publicly acknowledged Communist China's leadership of the Third World. With this Third World under China's leadership, he aligned the Philippines — right there in Peking, during his visit.

At the end of his visit, Mr. Marcos signed a joint communique which virtually absolved Communist China of ever attempting to subvert the Philippine government. The communique in part reads:

> The two governments agree that all foreign aggression and subversion and all attempts by any country to control another or to interfere in its internal affairs are to be condemned.

Very clearly, People's China categorically denied — and Mr. Marcos agreed — that China ever attempted to subvert the Philippine government. If China did, she would be virtually condemning herself in the very language of the Shanghai communique.

Premier Chou En-lai, in his very first meeting with Mr. Marcos, denied assisting the Philippine insurgents. He reminded his visitor that China had never violated the Bandung Principles, which called for peaceful co-existence and non-interference in another state's affairs. Mr. Marcos readily agreed with his host.

At the end of his visit, Mr. Marcos also agreed to exchange diplomatic missions with Communist China, thus establishing diplomatic relations and, in effect, severing diplomatic ties with Nationalist China. Mr. Marcos even went out of his way to turn over the Chinese Nationalist embassy on Roxas Boulevard to the Chinese communists — to the chagrin of the Taiwan government.

And so I ask once more: Which is the foreign power that I wanted to dominate and control our nation?

But there is an even greater defect in the charge. According to the Supreme Court's basic guidelines, the prosecution must prove that the accused joined the Communist Party of the Philippines, and in the case of any other subversive organization, that this subversive organization seeks to establish a totalitarian regime through violence and place it under the control and domination of a foreign power.

No witness that I can recall has ever testified that I am a member of the Communist Party of the Philippines and/or a subversive organization.

I challenge the prosecution to produce a single document showing my membership in the Communist Party of the Philippines and/or any subversive organization. The Armed Forces of the Philippines has captured tons and tons of communist literature, organizational charts, membership rosters and other vital documents. I challenge the prosecution or anyone to produce a single genuine communist document attesting to my membership in the Communist Party or any subversive organization.

The government claims to have captured the entire first echelon of command of the Communist Party of the Philippines and its military arm, the New People's Army. Many of the alleged leaders are in custody.

I challenge anyone, communist or non-communist, to testify that I "knowingly, feloniously, willfully and by overt acts conspired with them to overthrow the government of the Republic of the Philippines and/or any of its political subdivisions by force, violence, deceit, subversion or other illegal means; for the purpose of placing such government or political subdivisions under the control and domination of an alien power and establishing thereon a totalitarian regime," as the charge sheet indictment alleges.

I submit the government has charged me falsely and erroneously. And under the Supreme Court's basic guidelines, there is no way to convict me.

I will not even advance the proposition that RA 1700 as of June 11, 1975, has been impliedly repealed with the establishment of diplomatic relations with Communist China. Let others argue this point.

But I dare say that with the June 11, 1975 communique, Mr. Marcos accepted the Chinese leaders' disclaimer that People's China had ever tried to subvert the Philippine government!

Last year, Mr. Marcos journeyed to that other bastion of communism, the Soviet Union. At the end of his visit, he also signed a joint communique and agreed to establish diplomatic relations and exchange foreign missions. This last act should have sealed the fate of RA 1700, which was enacted in 1957 for the purpose of preventing our country from falling "under the control and domination of an alien power" — clearly the Soviet Union or People's China.

The main title of the Act is: "An Act to Outlaw the Communist Party of the Philippines and Similar Associations, Penalizing Membership Therein, and for Other Purposes." It has a shorter title. Section 1 provides, "This Act shall be known as the Anti-Subversion Act."

According to the Supreme Court decision:

> Together with the main title, the short title of the statute unequivocally indicates that the subject matter is SUBVERSION in general which has for its fundamental purpose the substitution of a foreign totalitarian regime in place of the existing government.

The Supreme Court ruled out the inclusion of democratic regimes like the United States or England or Malaysia, or even the anti-communist powers like Spain, Japan, Thailand or Taiwan, as possible alien powers in the context of the Act. The main thrust of the Act, according to the Supreme Court, is directed against a foreign communist power that is aiding the members of the Communist Party of the Philippines in its attempt to overthrow or subvert the government of the Philippines.

In fact, the Supreme Court categorically stated that the prosecution must prove that the Communist Party to which the accused belongs "is the same one outlawed by Congress in 1957 and it aims to overthrow the government by force, establish a totalitarian regime and place it under the control and domination of a foreign power." And in the case of a subversive organization, the Supreme Court ruled, the government must prove that the subversive organization aims to overthrow the government by force, establish a totalitarian regime and place the same under the control and domination of a foreign power.

The Philippines today has established diplomatic relations with almost all the communist states affiliated with the United Nations, and which are regarded as Soviet or Chinese satellites. There is hardly any foreign communist power left that may be accused of helping our local dissidents if we are to follow the logic of our diplomatic relations with the communist powers.

The usual practice is to break diplomatic relations — not establish them! — with states that you suspect are subverting your government.

If the Philippine government sincerely believes that the communist super-powers are supporting our dissidents, why did Mr. Marcos go out of his way to visit the capitals of communist powers, and establish relations with them?

I dare the prosecution, in the light of Mr. Marcos' latest diplomatic initiatives, to publicly accuse the People's Republic of China or the Soviet Union as the "foreign power" giving "active" and "material support" to local communist dissidents and subversives.

X

MY DUTY

**Accept whatever befalls you;
in crushing misfortune be patient;
For in fire gold is tested, and
worthy men in the crucible of humiliation.**

—ECCLESIASTICUS, 2:4-5

UMMATION:

Mr. President
Members of this Commission:

Our whole history as a people has been an epic struggle to end oppression and be free. In whole — and even in part — it ranks with the immortal stand made by Leonidas at the Pass of Thermopylae, the storming of the Bastille by the rebels of Paris, the Liberty-or-Death fight waged by the Thirteen American Colonies, the Defense of Britain by the English on nothing more than Winston Churchill's promise of "blood, toil, sweat and tears."

As a history, it has been as ennobling as it has been inspiring — washed, as it were, in the blood of our forebears, which gave it its glory and its purity, and sanctified, as we shall always recall proudly, with their lives, which gave it sterling nobility.

It is the supreme irony of our history that, having shaken off alien yokes, we now find ourselves groaning under a domestic yoke even more oppressive.

We are captives of a domestic tyranny that has outdone any and all of the foreign invaders in denying us our rights and liberties as men, and in the bestial fashion in which this was done.

So, we find ourselves again in a time of trials — a time that demands of each of us an unstinting, heroic response.

We must fight to regain our freedom. We cannot merely remain passive and wait for it to fall as a gift from heaven. For it is a futile hope, as the tyranny has shown us, to hope that it will come by the grace of the tyrant. Rather than give up martial rule, he will "institutionalize" it, as the tyrant himself has bluntly told us.

But, if we must be truly free, it must be a freedom never to be purchased at the cost of conviction and self-respect. Man must be ready — nay, willing! — to die if he cannot live as a free man. For freedom is never dear at any price. Truly, it is the breath of life.

And man's readiness to suffer — to die — will light the torch of freedom which can never be extinguished! No, not when it is in his heart and the hearts of his fellowmen!

It may not come today — or in his lifetime. But it will come, inexorably.

In any case, wherever such a man stands — be it in a tyrant's dungeon, where he makes his freedom's cry, or before a military tribunal, where he stands in righteous defiance — there, Mr. President, gentlemen of this Commission, there freedom stands. You cannot stifle it, much less kill it, with trumped-up charges, perjured witnesses, "evidence tortured into existence."

I find no need to affirm my innocence. In God's own season, the truth will be known.

My struggle is against a system of injustice that enables one man to judge the truth of his own accusations — to be the accuser, prosecutor and judge in a tribunal of his own creation; a court inescapably bound to follow his dictates.

My struggle is against a system that makes a mockery of justice by reducing all our judges to the status of hirelings, subservient to the will of the dictator.

My struggle is against a system that enables the dictator to own, control and manipulate — by himself or through his proxies — the mass media, so he can distort the truth, mislead the people by making vice appear as virtue and thereby weaken their resolve to be free.

My struggle is against a system that purports to promote the public welfare while enriching a few who shamelessly display the fruits of their greed and lust for wealth.

My struggle is against a system that not only enslaves our people but compel them to declare themselves for tyranny and their oppressor.

My struggle is against a system that pretends to save democracy while actually destroying it.

I have steadfastly refused to submit to the jurisdiction of a military commission as a matter of principle, even if by so refusing I permanently forfeit my physical freedom. My reason is simple: It is a basic right of every citizen to have a fair trial by a judiciary independent of executive control.

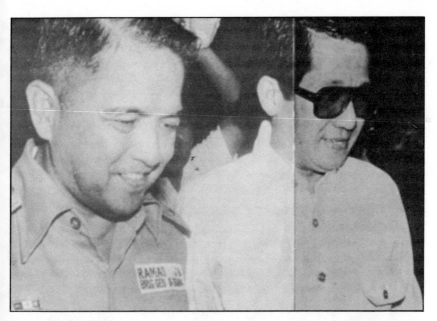

General Josephus Ramas escorting Ninoy during his departure for heart bypass operation in Dallas, Texas.

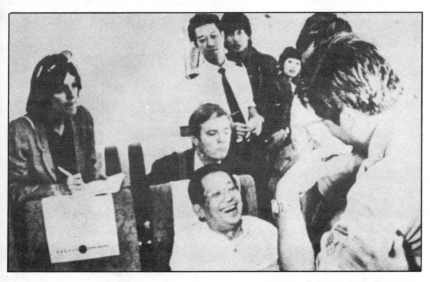

An unsuspecting Ninoy with all smiles at the military escort who fetched him up at the plane that took him back to the Philippines on Aug. 21, 1983.

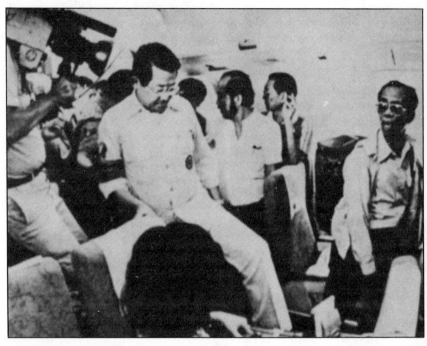

A television news cameraman covering Ninoy's arrival as he inches his way to the plane exit.

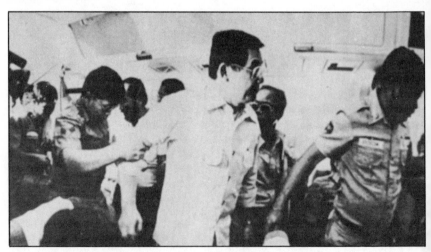

Military escorts obviously in a hurry to disembark with Ninoy.

Aside from myself, there are hundreds of other victims languishing in Marcos' prisons who, because of poverty, cannot avail of the service of competent legal counsel. It is also to share their plight that I am waging this struggle alone.

I believe that the Filipino people are perfectly capable of conducting their own affairs — of collectively arriving at decisions necessary for the security, peace and prosperity of this nation. They do not need a dictator to tell them what is good for them, or to force them into the mold of a so-called New Society which, far from being new, is as old as the tyranny of the Caesars.

Our people must exercise the sovereignty that is inalienably theirs. But this is precisely what the architect of the martial law regime persists in denying them.

They need freedom of speech and of the press. But how can there be such freedom when even the mildest discussion of public issues runs the risk of being penalized as subversive rumor-mongering punishable with imprisonment? When the media of mass communications are so rigidly controlled that factual information about matters in which our people have a vital interest is either withheld from them or spoonfed to them in diluted and distorted doses?

But then, no despot has ever succeeded in his purpose without the silent or passive acquiescence of his victims. History testifies that most people choose to yield to the will of a tyrant than to suffer the consequences of resistance. But it is equally true that even the most despotic government collapses when the people cease to fear its despotic force.

Strength does not come merely from physical force but more importantly from an indomitable will. The great Rizal said that there is no greater bravery than a resolute refusal to bend the knee to a tyrant, no matter how powerful the tyrant may be.

Our martyrs, in their time, sadly noted that repressed people are easily frightened by the slightest show of force and are unprepared for suffering and self-sacrifice. And so, not by words but by example did they show our people how to confront repression — not weakly and supinely but strongly and courageously. Truly, as shown by their example, men with faith can face martyrdom!

The scorching fires of my long years of isolation have literally forced me to seek the cool waters of the deep well of faith. And like Aeschylus, I have discovered "that even in our sleep pain which cannot forget falls drop by drop upon the heart, until in our despair against our will comes wisdom through the awful grace of God."

This wisdom brought me face to face with the truth: That truly we are only clay to be molded in the Potter's hands;

That not a blade of grass moves but by His will;

That He will save me if He needs me for further service — or further sacrifice. None can really take my life or save it against His will!

And like the apostle Paul, it was when I was weakest that I became strong, because for the first time I resigned myself completely to God's loving care. He protects and destroys, even if sometimes He destroys to protect.

With rebirth, my only prayer is to fade out doing my duty with my last breath.

But where lies my duty? What can a helpless detainee do to fight an entrenched tyranny? For a prisoner held in solitary confinement, prevented from communicating with the world, options for resistance are almost nil.

In my search for the right option, I came across the teachings of Gandhi — the great apostle of non-violent struggle, the *guru* who reminded the world of the great law of suffering and the tremendous strength of soul force.

Gandhi said:

> Non-violence in its dynamic condition means conscious suffering. It does not mean meek submission to the will of the evil doer but it means putting one's whole soul under the will of the tyrant. Working under this law of our being, it is possible for a single individual to defy the whole might of an unjust empire and lay the foundation for that empire's fall or its regeneration.

It was Gandhi who dramatically first employed the strategy of fasting and non-violent resistance. By fasting, he said, one allows violence to be done to one's self. And if he is wrong, only he suffers for his act. It aims to awaken in the tyrant a sense of shame and a renewal of his conscience from within.

The power of non-violence is that, in its own way and in its own time, it seeks to break the chain reaction of evil. To answer brutality with brutality is to admit one's moral and intellectual bankruptcy, and it can only start a vicious cycle. By refusing violent action, one does not permit the adversary to rationalize his own vindictive violence as self-defense.

I have fasted for forty days and forty nights, and I would like to believe that in some measure perhaps, I have hastened the ruling by the Supreme Court on two vital unprecedented issues. At least — to me — this has proved the validity of Gandhi's tragedy.

The tragedy of our time is that our people are faced by a double fear: the fear of the problem, which is the continuing tyranny; and the fear of the solution, which is the need to resist and suffer if need be with true courage.

Many of us have become like eunuchs: We know how to do it, but we cannot. We have lost our manhood.

My duty, as I see it, is to tell our people that we must not only dream of a good and just society. We must resolve to make this dream come true.

At the risk of being hated and despised, we must expose those despicable cowards in our midst who call themselves leaders while hiding behind the cloak of false prudence.

We must resolutely oppose those molders of public opinion who display such sycophancy as to put to shame those functionaries described in Suetonius' life of Tiberius.

Our people, especially the youth, seem to be sinking even deeper into an apolitical torpor. Far from welcoming the detachment of the young from social activism, we should take this as a terrible omen of a bleak future.

We must encourage the young to rise above a society that has been apathetic and indifferent and where justice has long been ignored. We must teach the young how to construct arguments, organize their thoughts, and turn their insights into ideas. They must develop true intellectual discipline and learn the meaning of moral courage.

They must acquire the moral fiber to support an indomitable will!

All of us must resolve to be true leaders who will reflect in the clearest way the aspirations of our people.

While, as I have said, I am surrendering my body, my spirit will never tolerate nor compromise with injustice, immorality and dictatorship. The spiritual man must put principles above expediency, duty above comfort, conscience above fleeting rewards, and God above the world.

I have made my decision. I have articulated the thoughts that have been bottled up in me for the last five years. I have done what I believe is my duty to do. I have wrested from life the joy and freedom to do what has to be done, speak what has to be spoken — leaving the consequences to God.

Harsh and bitter words have been uttered in the course of these proceedings. I have been branded an opportunistic politician, caricatured as a scoundrel, and, worse of all tagged as a conscienceless murderer and a subversive who planned to sell our country to an alien communist power.

But if one has been true to one's self, one can safely let the "turbid streams of rumor flow."

I pray that the seeds of thought that germinated in me — which I tried to nurture in my several statements — will eventually find fertile soil and bear fruit in the hearts and minds of my beloved countrymen.

I wish to acknowledge publicly the invaluable advice and moral support given me during those hours of crucial decision by my selfless legal advisers. I will never be able to match or repay their compassion and dedication.

I bow in humility to those co-workers who have kept faith — some of them enduring the unendurable, all of them risking their lives. I realize what they have gone through — and will still go through.

Hopefully, with the end of these proceedings, the woman who is the hope and light of my life's dark night will be delivered from her anxiety and anguish. She has stood by me with an unshakeable faith, unruffled and undeterred by the endless humiliations, the abandonment of friends, and the heavy burdens of having to be a teacher, father, mother and provider of my children. She has been the healing oasis in the desert of my prison.

I wish I had more than one life to give, for even if I had a hundred lives, I would never be able to repay the love and affection bestowed upon me by our great people — to whom, when I was desperate, I confided my despair; and with whom, when I was hopeful, I shared my hopes.

I end with the brave and noble refrain of our National Anthem:

Aming ligaya na pag may mang-aapi
ang mamatay ng dahil sa iyo.

APPENDICES

APPENDIX A

REPUBLIC OF THE PHILIPPINES
SUPREME COURT
MANILA

AURORA A. AQUINO
    Petitioner

- versus -   G.R. No. L-46909

MILITARY COMMISSION NO. 2,
    Respondent.
X ------------------------------------ X

MANIFESTATION

Comes now Petitioner, AURORA A. AQUINO, by undersigned counsel and unto this Honorable Supreme Court files the following manifestation, by incorporating and reproducing hereunder the letter addressed to the Supreme Court by her son, Benigno S. Aquino, Jr. recounting in detail the facts that transpired in the hearing last November 15, 1977 which in effect ignored and short-circuited the proceedings in the Supreme Court in the above entitled case.

SALONGA, ORDOÑEZ, YAP & ASSOCIATES
Rufino Building, Makati, Rizal

- and -

RAUL GONZALES
May Building, Manila

By: *[signature]*

JOVITO R. SALONGA

The Supreme Court
Manila

November 25, 1977
2300 Hours
MSU, Fort Bonifacio

The Chief Justice and Justices
Supreme Court of the Philippines

Sirs and Madam:

Thirty minutes ago, Military Commission No. 2 convicted and sentenced me together with PC Lt. Victor Corpuz and Bernabe Buscayno to die by firing squad.

I would like to bring to your attention what happened during the crucial thirteen hours that led to our death sentences in the hope that in the future you may prevent other hapless Filipinos from becoming victims of similar drumhead courts martial.

My worst fear of military "justice" is now reality. Procedural due process was violated with impunity. I was deceitfully silenced and effectively prevented from availing of the various options open to me under the Manual of Court Martial by the simple expedient of keeping me locked in my cell during the last vital eight hours of the proceedings.

> Why did Military Commission No. 2 deny our request to defer the hearings for a few days to allow the Supreme Court to decide our pending petitions?
>
> Why did the Military Defense Counsel who so diligently defended our rights up to July 22, 1977 suddenly ABANDONED US and became mysteriously tongue-tied and silent and never raised a single protest while our rights were being shamefully violated during the crucial thirteen hours.The tragedy of the situation was aggravated by the fact that I was kept out of the afternoon hearings leaving me totally unrepresented?
>
> Why was I prevented from returning to the hearings after the noon recess and brought back only to hear my conviction and sentence just before midnight?
>
> Why was I not allowed to read my statement as provided for in Manual of Court Martial or MCM Sec. 76?
>
> Why was I not allowed to make a closing argument? Why was I not asked, after the arguments and before the court closed to the findings, "whether I had anything further to offer" as provided for in Manual of Court Martial Sec. 77?

WHY THE INDECENT AND IMMORAL RUSH TO JUDGMENT?

Following, to the best of my recollection, is the chronological sequence of events that started at 0930 hours to 2230 hours, 25 November, 1977, the terrible thirteen hours that have brought us to the very jaws of death.

1. 0930 hrs: I was brought to Moran Hall, Fort Bonifacio to appear before Military Commission No. 2. After the commission convened, the trial Counsel announced the designation of a new Law Member, Lt. Col. Marciano I. Bacalla, vice Col. Salvador Sardalla. There having been no challenges (only a few clarificatory questions from civilian defense counsel Juan T. David) Brig. Gen. Jose Syjuco, president, administered the oath to Colonel Bacalla. The Trial Counsel then proceeded to brief the new Law Member.

2. 1015 hrs: Law Member Bacalla announced the commission has decided to rule on the three pending motions of the military defense counsel. Hearings recessed.

3. 1045 hrs: Hearing resumed and Law Member announced all Military Defense Counsel motions DENIED. The Law Member then proceeded to ask me whether I was ready to present evidence or witnesses for my defense. I said:

"I have a pending petition filed by my mother with the Supreme Court. I do not want to prejudice that case. I shall present evidence and witnesses for my defense AFTER THE SUPREME COURT SHALL HAVE DESIGNATED THE PROPER COURT TO HEAR MY CASE. Among other things, my petition questioned the capacity of this Commission to render fair and an impartial judgement in view of the uniqueness of my case."

The Law Member then interjected: "We take it you are not now ready to present any evidence or witness for your defense before this Commission?" To which I again replied: "I shall present evidence and witness for my defense after the Supreme Court shall have designated the proper court."

The Law Member then followed up with a second question. "Are you authorizing the military defense counsel to present any evidence or witness for your defense?" I answered: "The military defense counsel was appointed by the AFP Chief of Staff to defend all the accused before this Commission. I did not appoint him. He is not my counsel of choice. I can therefore neither authorize nor disauthorize him. All this time, he has been acting on his instructions from the AFP Chief of Staff."

4. 1100 hrs: After this brief question and answer period, the Law Member proceeded to rule: "This Commission rules that the case against Benigno S. Aquino, Jr. is deemed submitted." Without pausing, he then asked accused Bernabe Buscayno whether he was ready to present evidence or witness. Buscayno said, he also had a pending petition with the Supreme Court and wanted to await the High Court's ruling. There was some delay because of interpretation dif-

ficulties. Then Mr. Buscayno asked the court if his counsel of choice, Atty. Juan T. David, could speak for him. Atty. David said he had a pending motion to quash and/or a finding of not guilty and proceeded with his oral arguments.

I was stunned by the ruling of the commission that my case has been deemed submitted. While Atty. David was delivering his oral arguments, I asked the military defense counsel who was seated beside me whether he was still determined to defend as per his announcement last July 22, 1977. Lt. Col. Gonzalo T. Santos, the chief military counsel, could not respond and remained silent. He gave me the impression, he too was caught unaware by the suddenness of the commission ruling on my case. I SUDDENLY REALIZED I WAS ON MY OWN WITHOUT BENEFIT OF ANY COUNSEL.

Since August, 1976, the two military defense counsel: Lt. Col. Santos and Maj. Percival Pasion have been carrying the brunt of the defense after Lt. Corpuz and I announced after our arraignment that "we will not participate in the proceedings before Military Commission No. 2."

As late as July 22, 1977, the hearing before the fatal session, Military Defense Counsel Santos was categorically asked by Law Member Sardalla whether he was ready to introduce evidence for accused Aquino and Corpuz.

His answer appears on page 3 of the 22 July 1977 transcript:

"Yes, Your Honor. Notwithstanding his (Aquino) decision or that of Lt. Corpuz not to participate in these proceedings, as the duly designated Military Defense Counsel we believe that we are and should be made bound to discharge our duties accordingly. We will just defend the accused herein pursuant to our duties and responsibilities corollary and incident to our appointment as Military Defense Counsel."

When Law Member Bacalla announced the ruling that my case was deemed submitted, I expected the Military Defense Counsel to object and to proceed to present his evidence. Or at least, seek a reconsideration of his three denied motions. During the July 22, 1977 hearing the Military Defense Counsel categorically told the court that he needed only 21 days to prepare his evidence and witnesses for the defense. He even consulted me and asked for suggestions on possible witnesses. THE MILITARY DEFENSE COUNSEL REMAINED SILENT.

5. 1150 hrs: After Atty. David concluded his oral arguments, President Syjuco announced that the commission was going to retire and consider the David motion. He declared a recess and said hearings would be resumed at 1400 hours.

6. As Law Member Bacalla was leaving the Hall, I intercepted him to ask a few clarificatory questions. I wanted to know specifically if the commission has rescinded the previous ruling authorizing the Military Defense Counsel to pre-

sent evidence and witness for the accused. I wanted to know if the Military Defense Counsel has now been disauthorized to defend us and that we were STRICTLY ON OUR OWN. He asked me to direct my questions to President Syjuco. I therefore made the reservation that as soon as the hearings are resumed at 2 p.m. I would move for a reconsideration of the ruling and ask important clarificatory questions. I asked him whether the ruling that my case "is deemed submitted" meant that the commission can now deliberate on my case and proceed to convict and sentence me tonight or tomorrow. "Oh no," he said, "these hearings will still take some time because we still have to hear the defense of Buscayno and the commission cannot render any verdict till all cases have been heard." MY DISTINCT IMPRESSION FROM LAW MEMBER BACALLA WAS THAT THE HEARINGS WOULD STILL LAST AT LEAST ONE MORE WEEK. He assured me he will inform President Syjuco of our conversation. This conversation of mine with Law Member Bacalla proved to be my most fatal mistake, as subsequent events bore out. I WAS KEPT OUT OF THE AFTERNOON HEARINGS AND RETURNED ONLY FOR MY CONVICTION AND SENTENCING.

7. 1200 hrs: I was returned to the MSU compound where I have been detained for the last sixty months. I skipped lunch. I immediately re-read the Manual of Court Martial and brought out my previous notes and earlier transcripts of the proceedings.

Upon resumption of the hearings at 1400 hours I intended to bring out the following:

7.1 Under Manual of Court Martial (MCM) Sec. 71 (d), the defense, at the close of the case for the prosecution and before the opening of the case for the defense, may present a motion for a finding of not guilty. The court may rule upon the motion or defer action. I hurriedly prepared my notes for a motion for reconsideration of the denied defense motions for a finding of not guilty.

7.2 My motion for reconsideration will be made orally for lack of material time to reduce the same in writing. If my motion for reconsideration is denied, I intended to fall back on Manual of Court Martial Sec. 75 which provides that an accused may make an UNSWORN STATEMENT.

7.3 Manual of Court Martial Sec. 76 provides that the accused whether he has testified or not, may make an unsworn statement to the court in denial, explanation or extenuation of the offenses charged, but this right does not permit the filing of the accused's own affidavit. This statement is not evidence for he cannot be cross-examined upon it, but the prosecution may rebut statements of facts therein by evidence. Such consideration will be given the statement as the court deems warranted. This statement may be oral or in writing or both. A written statement should be signed and is ordinarily read to the court by the accused or by counsel.

I WAS READY WITH A 104-page STATEMENT which I prepared EARLY THIS YEAR AND WHICH HAS BEEN REPORTED BY THE PRESS!

7.4   My last option is the closing argument. According to Manual of Court Martial Sec. 77, after both sides have rested, arguments may be made to the court by the trial judge advocate, the accused, and his counsel. Arguments throughout the trial may be oral, in writing, or both except where the court requires an argument to be reduced in writing.

AFTER THE ARGUMENT AND BEFORE THE COURT CLOSES FOR THE FINDINGS, BOTH SIDES *SHOULD BE ASKED* WHETHER THEY HAVE ANYTHING FURTHER TO OFFER. (Manual of Court Martial Sec. 77)

After typing furiously for almost one hour and after collating my notes, I requested my military custodians to return me to Moran Hall before 1400 hours. I also requested that my Chief Legal Adviser Senator JOVITO SALONGA be contacted.

1400 hrs: My military custodians told me hearings delayed. I'll be brought to Moran Hall at 1500 hours.

1500 hrs: I was told Senator Salonga was contacted and has proceeded to Moran Hall. I inquired whether hearings have been resumed. "It is imperative that I attend the hearings to safeguard my rights," I told my military custodians.

1600 hrs: I felt like a caged animal in my hot and humid room. I was told my chief military custodian Lt. Melchor Acosta was at Moran Hall. I requested that if I could not be brought to Moran Hall, Senator Salonga be allowed to visit me here at MSU. My custodians promised to relay message to Lt. Acosta.

1700 hrs: I was getting desperate. No definite news from Moran Hall. When I again inquired about Senator Salonga, I was told he went home but that he would return to Moran Hall.

1800 hrs: I decided to undress and take a shower. I have not had breakfast and lunch. Every waiting minute was agonizing.

1900 hrs: Cryptic message came: BE READY AND STAND BY ON CALL.

2000 hrs: I asked if hearing resumed. NO NEWS, my custodians said. Just be ready and stand by.

2100 hrs: MY WORST FEARS WERE SLOWLY BECOMING REALITIES.

MY GUT FEELING SAYS I WILL BE CONVICTED AND SENTENCED WITHOUT ANY MORE CHANCE TO BE HEARD. I could not believe it was taking the commission more than nine hours to consider the DAVID motion when my three motions were disposed of in less than 20 minutes. Frantically, I pleaded with my military custodians to bring me back to Moran Hall. The response: Stand by on call!

2130 hrs: I am now sure my case was already being deliberated upon. To confirm this morbid thought, I inquired whether Lt. Corpuz has been alerted to return with us to Moran Hall. The answer of my custodians was an evasive denial. I DECIDED TO BRING OUT MY CHARCOAL GREY DENIM SUIT WHICH I ORDERED SPECIALLY FOR MY CONVICTION AND SENTENCING.

2200 hrs: STOIC RESIGNATION SETS IN. My military custodian informs me to be ready to go to Moran Hall "momentarily."

2205 hrs: I was led out of my detention room, brought to Moran Hall. Told to remain inside vehicle to allow commission members to enter first.

2210 hrs: Told to enter Moran Hall and stand in front of the Commission.

2215 hrs: Trial Counsel announced hearing resumed. Forthwith General Syjuco proceeded to read his prepared statement. Atty. David tried to raise a point of order. He was waived down by General Syjuco and went on to read our convictions and sentences.

2225 hrs: In less than 10 minutes General Syjuco finished reading our conviction and sentences. He then picked up his gavel, with a single tap declared the hearings adjourned and in quick fashion the entire commission filed out in brisk single file. Stunned by the swiftness of the event, we three accused looked at each other unbelieving if not amused, shook hands and were taken in tow by our respective military escorts.

2230 hrs: Back in my MSU cell to await final execution.

Your Honors: I am writing you this letter alone in my lonely cell. I have been sentenced to die by firing squad because I refused to participate in a proceeding which I consider a conscienceless mockery of justice. I have been deprived of my freedom and the company of my loved ones for the last 1,890 days. Now that the delayed shock has set in, I want to cry but I have no more tears to shed, my eyes have run dry over this long dark night.

I address you one last appeal—not for myself, but for persons similarly situated. Please put an end to drumhead courts martial and assert the independence of the judiciary if our Republic is to be saved.

I have always mistrusted military commissions. At the turn of the century, my own grandfather, Gen. Servillano Aquino was convicted and sentenced to death by musketry by an American military tribunal for alleged war crimes during the dying days of the Phil-American wars.

Our national hero, Dr. Jose Rizal was tried, convicted and sentenced by another military commission, set up by the Spanish colonial power. The tragedy may be mitigated because both, the one that sentenced my grandfather and Rizal to death, were alien military commissions.

If I have obstinately refused to yield to the tyranny of Mr. Marcos all these long years, if I have consistently denounced his usurpation, it is because I have not lost hope that sooner than later the Filipino's love for freedom will ultimately assert itself above the demands of temporary security and convenience.

A time comes in a man's life when he must take a stand and make a painful decision: to willingly die for his principles or surrender.

I have opted to die for my principles because my cause transcends my individual self and freedom. I am for a basic Human Right—the right of every citizen to a fair and an impartial trial by a Court of Law.

I urge you in the name of God and our people, to throw the full weight of your collective moral influence to restore the independence of the judiciary, the last bulwark of our freedom.

For the last four years, Mr. Marcos has been coercing me to defend myself before a kangaroo court of his own creation, composed of military officers directly under his control and supervision and whose careers he can advance, abort or destroy, on the very same charges which he himself, one full year before martial rule, described as "overwhelming."

My single, simple and consistent demand has been to be tried by an independent, authoritative and impartial court as due any citizen of a free Republic.

I am innocent of the charges levelled against me, but I would rather be shot by a firing squad than go through the motions of defending myself before a drumhead court martial and thus lend credibility to a farce and a mockery of justice.

Sincerely yours,

BENIGNO S. AQUINO, JR.

Ninoy's body sprawled on the tar-mac of the Manila International Airport near his alleged assassin.

Soldiers seemingly on alert while one of them lifts the body of Ninoy into the military van.

Cory, sprinkling holy water over the flag-draped casket of Ninoy.

APPENDIX B

AURORA A. AQUINO
    Petitioner

- versus -

G.R. No. L-46909
HABEAS CORPUS WITH
PRELIMINARY INJUNCTION

MILITARY COMMISSION NO. 2,
*SECRETARY OF NATIONAL
DEFENSE and CHIEF OF STAFF
OF THE ARMED FORCES OF THE
PHILIPPINES*

    Respondents.

X --------------------------X

SUPPLEMENTAL PETITION FOR HABEAS CORPUS, WITH APPLICATION FOR PRELIMINARY INJUNCTION AND/OR RESTRAINING ORDER EX PARTE

COMES NOW the Petitioner AURORA A. AQUINO, by her undersigned counsel and to his Honorable Supreme Court respectfully alleges:

1. That Petitioner is a widow, of legal age, Filipino citizen, and at present residing at 9 Masaya St., Quezon City; respondent Military Commission No. 2 is a military court vested with authority to administer military law among personnel of the military establishment, with offices at Fort Bonifacio, Makati, Metro Manila; respondent Juan Ponce Enrile is the incumbent Secretary of National Defense of the Republic of the Philippines, with office at Camp Aguinaldo, Quezon City; respondent Romeo Espino is the incumbent Chief of Staff of the Armed Forces of the Philippines, with office in Camp Aguinaldo, Quezon City.

2. That on September 14, 1977, Petitioner filed with the Honorable Supreme Court a petition for Habeas Corpus for the release from military custody and unlawful restraint of her son Benigno S. Aquino, Jr. who, as alleged in said petition, was denied the equal protection of the laws and should be released by above named respondents from all forms of restraint whatsoever; Petitioner further prayed that a writ of preliminary injunction or restraining order *ex parte* be issued by the Honorable Supreme Court while said petition for Habeas Corpus was pending in said court.

3. That on September 15, 1977, a writ of Habeas Corpus was issued by this Honorable Court which commanded the production of the body of said Benigno S. Aquino, Jr. before the Honorable Supreme Court; the respondents filed a Return to the writ, and after Petitioner had filed her Traversal of the Allegations in the Return, the said petition for Habeas Corpus was set for oral argument before the Honorable Supreme Court on October 18, 1977.

4. That during the oral argument of the said petition for Habeas Corpus on October 18, 1977, Petitioner was granted leave of court to file an Amended Petition for Habeas Corpus in order to include the respondent Secretary of National Defense and the respondent Chief of Staff among the respondents in the Petition, and this was promptly complied with by Petitioner on October 28, 1977 when a pleading entitled "Amendment Petition" was filed in the Supreme Court which alleged among others, that:

> "x x x *the Respondents Secretary of National Defense and Chief of Staff of the Armed Forces of the Philippines are hereby impleaded so that the fullest deliberation may be accorded to the plea of liberty by Petitioner's son* because they are the officers who act in behalf of the President of the Philippines under martial law and by whose authority petitioner's son is now detained, and both may be served with summons and other legal processes at their respective offices at Camp Aguinaldo, Quezon City;"

5. That the incident on October 18, 1977 which prompted the Honorable Supreme Court to grant leave of court to the Petitioner to include the Secretary of National Defense and the Chief of Staff among the respondents occurred when the Supreme Court asked the Solicitor General who was then arguing the case if the said pending resumption of hearing before respondent Military Commission No. 2 can be reset to a later date in order to enable the Supreme Court to resolve the issues raised in the petition for Habeas Corpus considering that it was the very jurisdiction of the respondent Military Commission which was in issue in said petition; Lt. Col. Juan Sison, specially designated military trial judge advocate in the case against Benigno S. Aquino, Jr. before said respondent Military Commission No. 2 was present in court at the time, and he was consulted by the Solicitor General if said trial before the respondent Military Commission No. 2 could be deferred while the Supreme Court was in the process of resolving the merits of the Petition for Habeas Corpus which squarely challenged the jurisdiction of Military Commission No. 2 to try Benigno S. Aquino, Jr. based on Petitioner's allegations that Benigno S. Aquino, Jr. had been denied the equal protection of the laws.

6. That after the said "consultation" in open court between the Solicitor General and Lt. Col. Juan Sison, the said proceedings before respondent Military Commission No. 2 were suspended until November 25, 1977 to enable the Supreme Court to decide on the merits the petition for Habeas Corpus which was then the

subject of oral argument before the Honorable Supreme Court.

7. That in a constitutionally untenable and arrogant display of naked power, in complete disregard of the agreement forged in the Supreme Court on October 18, 1977, the respondent Military Commission set the trial of Benigno S. Aquino, Jr. on November 25, 1977 and the most accurate account of the bizarre happening on that sad day for liberty can best be seen in the following narrative of Benigno S. Aquino, Jr. himself in his letter to the Supreme Court dated November 25, 1977:

"Following, to the best of my recollection, of the chronological sequence of events that started at 0930 hours to 2230 hours, 25 November, 1977, the terrible thirteen hours that have brought us to the very jaws of death.

1. 0930 hrs: I was brought to Moran Hall, Fort Bonifacio to appear before Miliary Commission No. 2. After the commission convened, the Trial Counsel announced the designation of a new Law Member, Lt. Col. Marciano I. Bacalla, vice Col. Salvador Sardalla. There having been no challenges (only a few clarificatory questions from civilian defense counsel Juan T. David) Brig. Gen. Jose Syjuco, president, administered the oath to Colonel Bacalla. The Trial Counsel then proceeded to brief the new Law Member.

2. 1015 hrs: Law Member Bacalla announced the commission has decided to rule on the three pending motions of the military defense counsel. Hearings recessed.

3. 1045 hrs: Hearing resumed and Law Member announced all Military Defense Counsel motions DENIED. The Law Member then proceeded to ask me whether I was ready to present evidence or witnesses for my defense.

   I said:
   "I have a pending petition filed by my mother with the Supreme Court. I do not want to prejudice that case. I shall present evidence and witnesses for my defense AFTER THE SUPREME COURT SHALL HAVE DESIGNATED THE PROPER COURT TO HEAR MY CASE. Among other things, my petition questioned the capacity of this Commission to render a fair and impartial judgement in view of the uniqueness of my case."

   The Law Member then interjected: "WE TAKE IT YOU ARE NOT NOW READY TO PRESENT ANY EVIDENCE OR WITNESS FOR YOUR DEFENSE BEFORE THIS Commission?" To which I again replied: "I shall present evidence and witness for my defense after the Supreme Court shall have designated the proper court."

   The Law Member then followed up with a second question. "Are you authorizing the military defense counsel to present any evidence or witness for your defense?" I answered: "The military defense counsel was appointed by the AFP Chief of Staff to defend all the accused before this Commission. I did not appoint him. He is not my counsel of choice. I can therefore neither authorize nor disauthorize him. All this time, he has been acting on his instructions from the AFP Chief of Staff."

4. 1100 hrs: After his brief question and answer period, the Law Member proceeded to rule: "This Commission rules that the case against Benigno S. Aquino, Jr. is deemed submitted." Without pausing, he then asked accused Bernabe Buscayno whether he was ready to present evidence or witness. Buscayno said, he also had a pending petition with the Supreme Court and wanted to await the High Court's ruling. There was some delay because of interpretation difficulties. Then Mr. Buscayno asked the court if his counsel of choice, Atty. Juan T. David, could speak for him. Atty. David said he had a pending motion to quash and/or a finding of not guilty and proceeded with his oral arguments.

I was stunned by the ruling of the commission that my case has been deemed submitted. While Atty. David was delivering his oral arguments, I asked the military defense counsel who was seated beside me whether he was still determined to defend as per his announcement last July 22, 1977. Lt. Col. Gonzalo T. Santos, the chief military counsel, could not respond and remained silent. He gave me the impression, he too was caught unaware by the suddenness of the commission ruling on my case. I SUDDENLY REALIZED I WAS ON MY OWN WITHOUT BENEFIT OF ANY COUNSEL.

Since August, 1976, the two military defense counsel: Lt. Col. Santos and Major Percival Pasion have been carrying the brunt of the defense after Lt. Corpuz and I announced after our arraignment that "we will not participate in the proceedings before Military Commission No. 2."

As late as July 22, 1977, the hearing before the fatal session, Military Defense Counsel Santos was categorically asked by Law Member Sardalla whether he was ready to introduce evidence for accused Aquino and Corpuz.

His answer appears on page 3 of the 22 July 1977 transcript:

'Yes, Your Honor. Notwithstanding his (Aquino) decision or that of Lt. Corpuz not to participate in these proceedings, as the duly designated Military Defense Counsel we believe that we are and should be made bound to discharge our duties accordingly. We will just defend the accused herein pursuant to our duties and responsibilities corollary and incident to our appointment as Military Defense Counsel.'

When Law Member Bacalla announced the ruling that my case was deemed submitted, I expected the Military Defense Counsel to object and to proceed to present his evidence. Or at least, seek a reconsideration of his three denied motions. During the July 22, 1977 hearing the Military Defense Counsel categorically told the court that he needed only 21 days to prepare his evidence and witnesses for the defense. He even consulted me and asked for suggestions on possible witnesses. THE MILITARY DEFENSE COUNSEL REMAINED SILENT.

5. 1150 hrs: After Atty. David concluded his oral arguments, President Syjuco announced that the commission was going to retire and consider the David motion. He declared a recess and said hearings would be resumed at 1400 hours.

6. As Law Member Bacalla was leaving the Hall, I intercepted him to ask him a few clarificatory questions. I wanted to know specifically if the commission has rescinded the previous ruling authorizing the Military Defense Counsel to present evidence and witness for the accused. I wanted to know if the Military Defense Counsel has now been disauthorized to defend us and that we were STRICTLY ON OUR OWN. He asked me to direct my questions to President Syjuco. I therefore made the reservation that as soon as the hearings are resumed at 2 p.m. I would move for a reconsideration of the ruling and ask important clarificatory questions. I asked him whether the ruling that my case "is deemed submitted" meant that the commission can now deliberate on my case and proceed to convict and sentence me tonight or tomorrow. "Oh no," he said, "these hearings will still take some time because we still have to hear the defense of Buscayno and the commission cannot render any verdict till all cases have been heard." MY DISTINCT IMPRESSION FROM LAW MEMBER BACALLA WAS THAT THE HEARINGS WOULD STILL LAST AT LEAST ONE MORE WEEK. He assured me he will inform President Syjuco of our conversation. This conversation of mine with Law Member Bacalla proved to be my most fatal mistake, as subsequent events bore out. I WAS KEPT OUT OF THE AFTERNOON HEARINGS AND RETURNED ONLY FOR MY CONVICTION AND SENTENCING.

7. 1200 hrs: I was returned to the MSU compound where I have been detained for the last sixty months. I skipped lunch. I immediately reread the Manual of Court Martial and brought out my previous notes and earlier transcripts of the proceedings.

Upon resumption of the hearings at 1400 hours I intended to bring out the following:

7.1 Under Manual of Court Martial (MCM) Sec. 71(d), the defense, at the close of the case for the prosecution and before the opening of the case for the defense, may present a motion for a finding of not guilty. The court may rule upon the motion or defer action. I hurriedly prepared my notes for a motion for reconsideration of the denied defense motions for a finding of not guilty.

7.2 My motion for reconsideration will be made orally for lack of material time to reduce the same in writing. If my motion for reconsideration is denied, I intended to fall back on Manual of Court Martial Sec. 75 which provides that an accused may make an UNSWORN STATEMENT.

Manual of Court Martial Sec. 76 provides that the accused whether he has testified or not, may make an unsworn statement to the court in denial, explanation or extenuation of the offenses charged, but this right does not permit the filing of the accused's own affidavit. This statement is not evidence for he cannot be cross-examined upon it, but the prosecution may rebut statements of facts therein by evidence. Such consideration will be given the statement as the court deems warranted. This statement may be oral or in writing or both. A written statement should be signed and is ordinarily read to the court by the accused or by counsel.

I WAS READY WITH A 104-page STATEMENT which I prepared EARLY THIS YEAR AND WHICH HAS BEEN REPORTED BY THE PRESS!

7.3   My last option is the closing argument. According to Manual of Court Martial Sec. 77, after both sides have rested, arguments may be made to the court by the trial judge advocate, the accused, and his counsel. Arguments throughout the trial may be oral, in writing, or both, except where the court requires an argument to be reduced in writing.

AFTER THE ARGUMENT AND BEFORE THE COURT CLOSES FOR THE FINDINGS, BOTH SIDES *SHOULD BE ASKED* WHETHER THEY HAVE ANYTHING FURTHER TO OFFER. (Manual of Court Martial Sec. 77)

8. After typing furiously for almost one hour and after collating my notes, I requested my military custodians to return me to Moran Hall before 1400 hours. I also requested that my Chief Legal Adviser Senator JOVITO SALONGA be contacted.

9 . 1400 hrs: My military custodians told me hearings delayed. I'll be brought to Moran hall at 1500 hours.

1500 hrs: I was told Senator Salonga was contacted and has proceeded to Moran Hall. I inquired whether hearings have been resumed. "It is imperative that I attend the hearings to safeguard my rights," I told my military custodians.

1600 hrs: I felt like a caged animal in my hot and humid room. I was told my chief military custodian Lt. Melchor Acosta was at Moran Hall. I requested that if I could not be brought to Moran Hall, Senator Salonga be allowed to visit me here at MSU. My custodians promised to relay message to Lt. Acosta.

1700 hrs: I was getting desperate. No definite news from Moran Hall. When I again inquired about Senator Salonga, I was told he went home but that he would return to Moran Hall.

1800 hrs: I decided to undress and take a shower. I have not had breakfast and lunch. Every waiting minute was agonizing.

1900 hrs: Cryptic message came: BE READY AND STAND BY ON CALL.

2000 hrs: I asked if hearing resumed. NO NEWS, my custodians said. Just be ready and stand by.

2100 hrs: MY MOST WORST FEARS WERE SLOWLY BECOMING REALITIES. MY GUT FEELING SAYS I WILL BE CONVICTED AND SENTENCED WITHOUT ANYMORE CHANCE TO BE HEARD. I could not believe it was taking the commission more than nine hours to consider the DAVID motion when my three motions were disposed of in less than 20 minutes. Frantically, I pleaded with my military custodians to bring me back to Moran Hall. The response: Stand by on call!

2130 hrs: I am now sure my case was already being deliberated upon. To confirm this morbid thought, I inquired whether Lt. Corpuz has been alerted to return with us to Moran Hall. The answer of my custodians was an evasive denial. I DECIDED TO BRING OUT MY CHARCOAL GREY DENIM SUIT WHICH I ORDERED SPECIALLY FOR MY CONVICTION AND SENTENCING.

2200 hrs: STOIC RESIGNATION SETS IN. My military custodian informs me to be ready to go to Moran Hall "momentarily."

2205 hrs: I was led out of my detention room, brought to Moran Hall. Told to remain inside vehicle to allow commission members to enter first.

2210 hrs: Told to enter Moran Hall and stand in front of the Commission.

2215 hrs: Trial Counsel announced hearing resumed. Forthwith General Syjuco proceeded to read his prepared statement. Atty. David tried to raise a point of order. He was waived down by General Syjuco and went on to read our convictions and sentences.

2225 hrs: In less than 10 minutes General Syjuco finished reading our conviction and sentences. He then picked up his gavel, with a single tap declared the hearings adjourned and in quick fashion the entire commission filed out in brisk single file. Stunned by the swiftness of the event, we three accused looked at each other unbelieving if not amused, shook hands and were taken in tow by our respective military escorts.

2230 hrs: Back in my MSU cell to await final execution."

8. That in utter disregard of the manifestation of Benigno S. Aquino, Jr. that he desires to await the decision of the Supreme Court on the Petition for Habeas Corpus which his mother, Petitioner herein, had filed in the Supreme Court which seeks the absolute release of Benigno S. Aquino, Jr. from all forms of confinement or restraint because he was denied the equal protection of the laws, the said respondent Military Commission callously proceeded to try Benigno S. Aquino, Jr., prodded by military prosecutor Lt. Col. Juan Sison who was present in the

Supreme Court on October 18, 1977 when the agreement to suspend the proceedings before the Military Commission was reached to enable the Supreme Court to decide the pending petition for Habeas Corpus, resulting in a VERDICT OF DEATH BY MUSKETRY against Benigno S. Aquino, Jr. and his co-accused.

9. That the display of hostility by the respondent Military Commission against Benigno S. Aquino, Jr. as narrated above emphasizes the inherent inability of Military Commission No. 2 to administer justice in a dispassionate and an impartial manner, and unless the same is rectified by the equitable processes of the Supreme Court, Benigno S. Aquino, Jr. will be denied the equal protection of the laws, and that unless the Honorable Supreme Court "lays the law" on the respondent Military Commission No. 2, the law of the land will no longer be the Bill of Rights in the Constitution as protected by the Supreme Court under its power of judicial review, but the will of the military running riot under color of law, insensitive to the command of the constitution, unheeding of the rule of law, not even condescending to the Honorable Supreme Court.

10. That the wanton act of respondent Military Commission which brought Benigno S. Aquino, Jr. so near the firing squad has blighted the life of Benigno S. Aquino, Jr. and any further proceedings against him now will place him in jeopardy of being punished for the same offense; a mere reversal of the atrocious proceedings in the respondent Military Commission can not restore what has been taken away from him—his peace of mind, his hope in the sense of justice of those who will pass judgment on him, and his right to the presumption of innocence.

11. That Petitioner submits that the unjustified act of the respondent Military Commission in ordering that the case against Benigno S. Aquino, Jr. be considered submitted for decision notwithstanding the fact that Benigno S. Aquino, Jr. was then ready to make his closing statement in the face of the refusal of his military defense counsel to make the said closing statement for him, constituted a substantial violation of his right to due process and that any further proceedings against him before respondent Military Commission will amount to his being tried and being placed in jeopardy again for the same offense, a right which Petitioner is now invoking pursuant to Section 9, Rule 117 of the Rules of Court of the Philippines which reads as follows:

"Section 9. Former conviction or acquittal or former jeopardy. When a defendant shall have been convicted or acquitted, or the case against him dismissed or otherwise terminated without the express consent of the defendant, by a court of competent jurisdiction, upon a valid complaint or information or other formal charge sufficient in form and substance to sustain a conviction, and after the defendant had pleaded to the charge, the conviction or acquittal of the defendant or the dismissal of the case shall be a bar to another prosecution for the same offense charged, or for any attempt to commit the same or frustration thereof, or for any offense which necessarily included in the offense charged in the former complaint or information."

13. That Petitioner's contention that her son Benigno S. Aquino, Jr. will be placed in double jeopardy if he were to be tried again by the respondent Military Commission finds support in the case of United States vs. Robert L. Mathis, ACM-S3514 reported in 21 Court Martial Reports, p. 661, where the following was held:

"....the right of counsel implies the right of effective assistance throughout the 'entire proceedings.' The right to this assistance 'cannot be satisfied by mere formal appointment...The right of counsel is so fundamental that encroachment thereupon constitutes a lack of due process of law which cannot be cured by clear and compelling evidence of guilt...

"The president of the court instructed the court on the elements of consummated assault. Subsequently, the president denied defense counsel his request to give closing argument. In adjudging a sentence the court imposed substantially the maximum permissible for the offense charged, including a bad conduct discharge. Held: Denial of such request was an abuse of sound discretion and was prejudicial to the accused's substantial rights."

14. That in rushing a judgement of conviction on Benigno S. Aquino, Jr. without making a formal resolution of denial of his Motion for a Finding of Not Guilty in all the cases against him, the respondent Military Commission betrayed its lack of a judicial mind which renders it incompetent to try Benigno S. Aquino, Jr.; the important legal grounds stated by him in said three motions for a Finding of Not Guilty were arbitrarily disposed of by the statement that "there is sufficient evidence in order to convict the accused" because of its predisposition to find Benigno S. Aquino, Jr. guilty. For example, the legal question of whether he can be convicted under a decree or law on illegal possession of firearms which makes it punishable by death that was promulgated after his arrest cannot be arbitrarily disposed of by merely stating, as respondent Military Commission did, that "there is sufficient evidence in order to convict the accused." Again, the question of whether there should be only one case for subversion instead of splitting up into so many separate charges cannot be disposed of by such a similar ruling. Similarly, the question of whether an alleged expert can testify on the question of "whether Benigno S. Aquino, Jr. is a subversive in his opinion" cannot be disposed of by such a capricious ruling.

15. That in rushing a judgement of conviction that Benigno S. Aquino, Jr. should be shot by a firing squad after denying the right of Benigno S. Aquino, Jr. to give his closing argument when his assigned counsel failed to give him an effective legal assistance, the respondent Military Commission showed its inherent inability to dispense justice, hence it should be restrained from trying Benigno S. Aquino, Jr.

16. That the act of the Commander-in-Chief of the Armed Forces of ordering the reopening of the proceedings against Benigno S. Aquino Jr. before the respondent Military Commission even before the records of the proceedings were officially indorsed to him by the respondent Military Commission, and the alacrity with which said respondent responded by setting the resumption of proceedings on Monday, December 5, 1977, unmistakeably belies the pretension of the Commander-in-Chief that the respondent is an independent body whose performance of duty was not within the control or supervision of the Commander-in-Chief and, furthermore, plainly proves the abject subservience of respondent commission to the wishes of the Commander-in-Chief of the Armed Forces who has earlier repeatedly declared that Benigno S. Aquino, Jr. is guilty of all the charges against him.

17. That if indeed the judgment of respondent Military Commission that Benigno S. Aquino, Jr. has been sentenced TO DIE BEFORE A FIRING SQUAD is not a judgment of conviction but technically a mere recommendation, still such sentence is entitled to very great weight and cannot be legally ignored or disregarded even by the reviewing authority; no new matter can be injected nor can the record be changed in any way or manner.

18. That in order to avoid more hasty and arbitrary action by respondent Military Commission, Petitioner and her counsel filed with the Honorable Supreme Court an Urgent Motion for Leave to File Supplemental Pleading on November 28, 1977 and leave of court was granted on November 29, 1977; in accordance with said leave of court, the present supplemental Petition for Habeas Corpus, With Prayer for Writ of Preliminary Injunction and/or Restraining Order Ex Parte has been filed by the Petitioner.

19. That the petition for Habeas Corpus which Petitioner has filed in the Supreme Court and which she later amended as alleged above in accordance with the agreement between Petitioner's counsel and the Solicitor General on October 18, 1977 is neither capricious nor whimsical, as may be seen from the following allegations which are re-pleaded from the original amended petition, omitting the annexes thereto which maybe considered as integral parts of this petition whose markings will remain unchanged for the purposes of this Supplemental Petition.

20. That Petitioner is filing this petition for Habeas Corpus in behalf of her son, Benigno S. Aquino, Jr., who is now detained in Fort Bonifacio, Makati, Metro Manila, under the custody of respondent Military Commission under circumstances which deny her son the equal protection of the laws, in gross violation of the constitutional right of said Benigno S. Aquino, Jr., as will hereafter be narrated.

21. That the issue of deprivation of the equal protection of the laws whenever presented by an individual who lives under the aegis of constitutional government,

presents a justiciable controversy over which the Honorable Supreme Court has jurisdiction, in accordance with the language of Senior Justice Enrique Fernando in his dissenting and concurring opinion in *Aquino vs. Ponce Enrile,* 59 SCRA (1974):

> "It may happen though that officers of lesser stature not impressed with a high sense of responsibility would utilize the situation to cause the apprehension of person without justification. Certainly it would be to my mind to sanction oppressive acts if the validity of such detention cannot be inquired into through habeas corpus. It is more than just desirable therefore that if such be the intent, there be a specific decree concerning the suspension of the writ of habeas corpus. Even then, however, such proclamation can be challenged. If vitiated by constitutional infirmity, the release may be ordered."

22. The above quoted view on the justiciability of the question of habeas corpus in a martial law setting is shared by other justices of this Honorable Supreme Court. Thus, the then Chief Justice Makalintal stated in *Aquino vs. Ponce Enrile,* supra:

> "Arrayed on the side of justiciability are Justice Castro, Fernando, Teehankee and Muñoz Palma. x x x on this point the Court is practically unanimous."

23. That the justiciability of the controversy presented by this petition for Habeas Corpus is not barred by any order or decree of the President of the Philippines.

24. That this petition for Habeas Corpus is premised on the legal right of Petitioner to seek the release of her son, Benigno S. Aquino, Jr., from all forms of unlawful restraint committed against him by respondent Military Commission, in accordance with Section 3 of Rule 102 of the Rules of Court which provides as follows:

> "Sec. 3, Rule 102. Requisites of application therefore. - Application for the writ shall be by petition signed and verified either by the party for whose relief it is intended, or by some person on his behalf..."

25. That the allegations of this Petition for Habeas Corpus which seeks the release of Benigno S. Aquino, Jr. from unlawful detention in the custody of respondent Military Commission have not been passed upon by this Honorable Supreme Court in any prior petition for the release of said Benigno S. Aquino, Jr.; although Benigno S. Aquino, Jr. had filed an earlier petition for habeas corpus which was docketed as G.R. No. L-35546, Sept. 17, 1974, 59 SCRA 183 and which was dismissed by this Honorable Supreme Court, the said tribunal did not foreclose the possibility that Benigno S. Aquino, Jr. might be released from unlawful restraint of his liber-

ty if his continued detention at some point in time can be shown to be in violation of his constitutional rights. We quote below the view of Senior Justice Fernando on this point:

> "It is likewise my submission that even if the validity of the proclamation is sustained and the doubt is removed as to such individuals having been deprived of the privilege of the writ, still *if their preventive detention after an extended period of time may assume a punitive aspect,* they may again invoke the writ with the end in view of making out a case of unconstitutional application as to them of such martial law proclamation. If successful, they may be able to regain their liberty. What is more, they may be able to show *that circumstances have so changed* that the continuance of martial law itself may be tainted with a degree of arbitrariness. Even then, the executive determination is of course impressed with the greatest weight, and ordinary deference must be shown. Nonetheless, and this to my mind is crucial, such an opportunity should not be denied petitioners and habeas corpus is the appropriate remedy, the bar of the alleged suspension of the privilege as to the persons detained being unavailing under the circumstances." "The Writ of Liberty Under Martial Law: Malcolm on Habeas Corpus Revisite" by Enrique M. Fernando, in volume 50, Philippine Law Journal, July, 1975, No. 3, p. 295). (Underscoring supplied)

26. That Petitioner alleges that the continued detention by respondent Military Commission of Benigno S. Aquino, Jr. in the light of facts and events which have taken place after his first petition for habeas corpus mentioned above denied him the equal protection of the laws.

27. That under military rules of procedure, once the charges against Benigno S. Aquino, Jr. are filed with respondent Military Commission No. 2, said commission assumes full responsibility for his detention. On this point, in an article entitled "Administration of Justice by the Military", written by Col. Vicente Pascual, Deputy Judge Advocate General of the Armed Forces of the Philippines, published in the Journal of the Integrated Bar of the Philippines, Vol. 4, Nos. 3 & 4, p. 182, the following fundamental rule in the administration of military justice is emphasized:

> "The legal custody over a person facing a criminal charge before a military court is vested in the court itself who may specify the type of his restraint while pending trial. Thereafter, and while awaiting final result of trial, legal custody over him is vested in the reviewing authority." Vol. 4, Nos. 3 & 4, Journal of the Integrated Bar of the Phil. 187.

28. That the continued assertion by respondent Military Commission No. 2 of exclusive jurisdiction to try Benigno S. Aquino, Jr. constitutes a denial of the equal protection of the laws because Muslim rebels who have taken up arms against the government and who, since before the proclamation of martial law, have in-

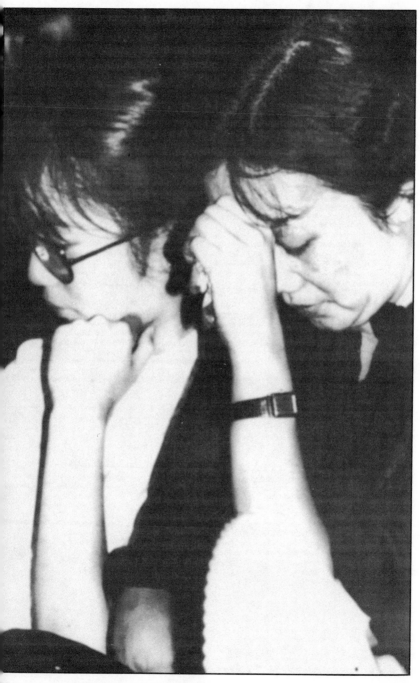

Grieving daughter Kris and Cory.

I AM BENIGNO S AQUINO JR., 43, Filipino, married, father of five, a native of Concepcion, Tarlac and presently detained - since September 23, 1972 - at the MSU compound of the Philippine Army at Fort Binifacio.

My detention camp is also known as the "cemetery for the living" ~~to distinguish~~ to distinguish it from the America War Dead Memorial Cemetery directly to the north of it and the Libingan Ng Mga Bayani, slightly to the south of it.

I am a third generation of public servants jailed for serving the Filipino people.

I am the grandson of the late General Serviliano Aquino of the Filipino Revolutionary Army under President Aguinaldo of the First Republic. Shortly after the turn of the century, my grandfather was captured by American occupying forces, tried, convicted and sentenced to death by an American Military Tribunal for "guerilla war crimes even after the capitulation of President Aguinaldo." He escaped execution only after President Theodore Roosevelt declared an amnesty for all Filipino rebels. For six years, my grandfather was imprisoned in the dungeons of Fort Santiago.

I am the son of the late BENIGNO S AQUINO Sr., a former congressman, a senator (majority floor leader) and cabinet member under President Quezon during the Philippine Commonwealth. ~~During the second world war, he became the Speaker of the National Assembly and was~~ the No. 2 man ~~~~ of the wartime Second Republic. ~~For his wartime services to the ~~~~ Filipino people,~~ American authorities imprisoned my father, together with the other members of the wartime government in exile, in Tokyo's Sugamo Prison. ~~~~ He regained his freedom at the birth of the Third Republic, when ~~the then President Manuel L. Roxas declared an amnesty for all those who served in the wartime government. Like my father, President Roxas also served the Laurel wartime government as the Rice Czar.~~

A am a product of the Benedictine and Jesuit ratio studiorum. After twelve years in catholic educational institutions, I took up law at the University of the Philippines.

I am a former newspaperman (The Manila Times). At 17, I was a war correspondent (Korea). Later, I became a foreign correspondent (Indo-China, Malaya, Indonesia and the Middle East). In 1955, I was elected as mayor of Concepcion, Tarlac. In 1959, I was elected ~~~~ vice governor of Tarlac province. In 1961, I became governor of Tarlac province. I was elected to the same office in 1963. In 1967, I was elected to the Senate of the Philippines.

I was executive assistant to three former Presidents: Magsaysay Garcia and Macapagal. I was awarded decorations by three Presidents: Quirino (The Philippine Legion of Honor, degree of officer for services during the Korean War); Magsaysay (the Philippine Legion of Honor, degree of Commander for negotiating the return to the government of Luis M. Taruc, erstwhile Huk Supremo in 1954); Gar

Facsimile of a page from Ninoy's manuscript

flicted and still inflict heavy losses and casualties on men and material of the Armed Forces of the Philippines are entitled to complete amnesty and release by virtue of paragraph 12 (a) and (b) of the Tripoli Agreement of December 23, 1976 between the Government of the Republic of the Philippines and the Moro National Liberation Front (MNLF), copy of which is hereto attached as Annex "A" and made an integral part of this petition, and which, in part, provides as follows:

> "12) Cease fire shall be declared immediately after the signature of this agreement provided that its coming into effect shall not exceed the 20th January 1977. A Joint Committee shall be composed of the two parties with the help of the Organization of the Islamic Conference represented by the Quadripartite Ministerial Commission to supervise the implementation of the ceasefire.
>
> The said Joint Committee shall also be charged with supervising the following:
>
> a. A complete amnesty in the areas of the autonomy with the renunciation of all legal claim . . . resulting from events which took place in the South of the Philippines.
>
> b. The release of all political prisoners who had relations with events in the south of the Philippines."

29. That from the time said Tripoli Agreement was entered into, no Muslim rebel carrying firearms or committing any act of subversion or rebellion has been or is being prosecuted for illegal possession of firearms, subversion, or rebellion.

30. That the continued adherence of the Philippines to the said Tripoli Agreement up to the date of the filing of this Petition for Habeas Corpus is officially acknowledged by the government of the Republic of the Philippines; for instance, Defense Undersecretary Carmelo Z. Barbero who signed the Tripoli Agreement, on behalf of the Philippine Government, declared in a speech before the Manila Rotary Club on September 8, 1977 that the ceasefire provision in the said agreement was being observed by the Armed Forces but was being violated because of abuses committed by the MNLF rebels;

> "Defense Undersecretary Carmelo Z. Barbero expressed fears yesterday that the time may come when members of the Armed Forces may no longer be able to control their temper over abuses committed by rebels in the south, the ceasefire agreement notwithstanding.
>
> On this note, Barbero, who is co-chairman of the national ceasefire committee, called upon Nur Misuari, chairman-in-exile of the Moro National Liberation Front (MNLF), to return to the Philippines and "personally lead and conduct his followers properly."

Excerpt of said speech which was published in the Bulletin Today issue on

September 9, 1977, is attached to this petition as Annex "B".

31. That respondent Military Commission No. 2 is now implementing a publicly announced policy of the military establishment which requires the transfer of authority to try civilians under indictment before military courts to civil courts; clearly, then, such policy is prompted by the conviction that civil courts can administer justice in an orderly and dispassionate manner; copy of Department Order No. 95 issued on July 16, 1977 entitled "Guidelines on the Transfer to the Civil Courts of Cases of Accused Who Have Been Arraigned" is attached to this Petition as Annex "C", and made an integral part hereof, and which, for convenience, is quoted below:

"1. The transfer of the said cases to the proper civil court may be ordered by the military tribunal concerned, only under the following conditions:

a) Upon written or oral motion of the accused praying that this case, notwithstanding that he has been arraigned and pleaded to the charge or charges, should be transferred to the proper civil court for continuation of trial;

b) The motion for transfer should be made by the accused within thirty (30) days, (1) after having been advised by the military tribunal trying him that, pursuant to this Order, he may request for the transfer of his case from the military tribunals to the civil courts, or (2) from receipt by him and/or his counsel of record from the military tribunal of a copy of this Order; and

c) The prosecution must not have presented substantial evidence establishing, or tending to establish, the guilt of the accused.

2. To pre-empt any future legal move of the accused to raise the question of former jeopardy, he should be asked to sign his conformity at the bottom of the Order of the court directing the transfer of the case to the proper civil court. For example: "WITH MY CONFORMITY/EXPRESSED CONSENT";   *

_____

                                      Accused

3. The complete record of the court proceedings in this regard, and the Order of the Court itself, should form part of the records of the case to be transferred to the civil court.

4. Upon the grant by the military tribunal of the motion of the accused for the transfer of his case to the proper civil court, the military tribunal shall forthwith transmit the complete record of the case, to include all evidence in the case, to the Judge Advocate General, AFP (Attn: Clerk of Military Tribunals) who will undertake the actual transfer of the record of the case to the proper civil court."

32. That as of August 12, 1977, the military tribunals of the Armed Forces of

the Philippines have reportedly indorsed to civilian courts for trial approximately 3146 cases, as per public announcement published on August 13, 1977, in the *Daily Express,* a metropolitan newspaper; copy of said public announcement is attached to this Petition as Annex "D" and which in part states as follows:

> "A TOTAL OF 1,867 more cases was approved yesterday for transfer from the military to the civil courts in compliance with the decrees issued recently by President Marcos.
>
> "Brig. Gen. Hamilton B. Dimaya, judge advocate general of the Armed Forces, recommended yesterday to Defense Secretary Juan Ponce Enrile the transfer of the cases after a coordinating conference with civilian law officials led by Supreme Court Justice Guillermo Santos.
>
> "Dimaya, as AFP judge advocate general, will determine if any case involving a civilian will be referred to a military tribunal for trial. Actual referral, however, shall be made only with the written approval of the defense chief.
>
> "The AFP judge advocate general is also authorized to dismiss cases with purely civilian respondents where the evidence is determined by him to be insufficient to sustain a prima facie finding.
>
> Since the department order went into effect last June 17, Dimaya has ordered the dismissal of 1,221 cases involving 2,248 respondents.
>
> LAWYERS of the AFP judge advocate general's office had earlier referred to the civil courts 1,279 cases involving 3,142 respondents.
>
> A total of 2,366 cases, however, are expected to be retained for trial by military tribunals.
>
> These cases deal with offenses committed by military personnel, crimes against national security, violations of the Anti-Subversion Law, espionage, crimes against public order as defined and penalized under the Revised Penal Code, violations of the laws on firearms and explosives, crimes as defined and penalized under Presidential Decree No. 33 (such as printing, possession, distribution and circulation of certain leaflets, handbills, and propaganda materials, and the inscribing of grafitti), and usurpation of military authority, rank, title and the illegal manufacture, sale or use of military uniforms and insignia as embraced in Articles 179 and 177 of the Revised Penal Code and in Republic Act No. 493.

33. That the classification or enumeration of those cases which shall be tried by military court such as respondent Military Court No. 2, as set apart from those which shall be tried by civil courts stated in the "Guidelines" attached hereto as Annex "A", is grossly discriminatory to Benigno S. Aquino, Jr. especially because the retention of jurisdiction over the charges against Benigno S. Aquino, Jr. is made to rest upon the uncontrolled, arbitrary discretion of respondent Military Commission itself, and this is shown by the fact that said "Guidelines" require that:

> "The motion for transfer should be made by the accused within thirty (30) days,
> (1) after having been advised by the military tribunal trying him that, pursuant to this Order, he may request for the transfer of his case from the military tribunals to the civil courts..." (paragraph 1 (b) of Guidelines).

34. That in view of the actuations of respondent Military Commission No. 2,

such an advise by the military tribunal trying him is not only unlikely but impossible; in fact, respondent Military Commission No. 2 has required Benigno S. Aquino, Jr. to present his evidence on September 19, 1977.

35. That the classification or enumeration of those cases which shall be tried by military courts including respondent Military Commission No. 2 is arbitrary and unreasonable because it vests jurisdiction over offenses committed by civilians involving acts which were not triable by any military court or tribunal prior to the creation of respondent Military Commission No. 2 and this discrimination constitutes a usurpation by respondent Military Commission of the constitutional functions of civil courts, in view of the fundamental change in circumstances obtaining today.

36. That the proceedings before respondent Military Commission No. 2 have denied Benigno S. Aquino, Jr. the equal protection of the laws, in that:

a. Notwithstanding the rule laid down in People v. Hernandez, 99 Phil. 515, to the effect that separate acts of arson and murder, when done in furtherance of the rebellion, are absorbed in the single offense of rebellion and for which a single penalty may be imposed, respondent Commission, over the repeated objections of Military Defense Counsel for Benigno S. Aquino, Jr., has permitted and sanctioned the prosecution of said accused for four (4) separate cases of subversion (Crim. Cases Nos. MC-2-20, MC-2-21, MC-2-23 and MC-2-24), which in itself is unconscionable and illegal, and the further prosecution of said accused for murder (MC-2-22) and illegal possession of firearms (Crim. Cases Nos. MC-2-19) all of which should have been considered as absorbed in a single case of subversion in light of Prosecution's own theory that accused Aquino was motivated in all these alleged offenses to subvert the Government of the Republic of the Philippines.

b. *With respect to the charges of subversion, of the twenty two (22) witnesses presented by the prosecution, eleven (11) witnesses confessed in open court that they have been members of the NPA/CPP or the HMB and actively worked for these subversive organizations in various ways. All these witnesses, except Commanders Melody and Pusa, are free and unlike accused Benigno S. Aquino, Jr, they have never been charged before any court for their admitted crimes. Commanders Melody and Pusa were similarly charged, but notwithstanding their confessions of guilt, including the killing of many people, they were later freed and utilized as state witnesses. Thereafter, said persons died mysteriously.*

37. The denial of the equal protection of the laws is further shown by the following circumstances which are within the scope of judicial knowledge or are capable of unquestionable demonstration:

a. Benigno S. Aquino, Jr. is now prosecuted for alleged illegal possession of firearms, yet Muslims who are known to possess firearms are rewarded by granting to them bank loans up to P5,000.00 each without collateral provided they surrender their firearms; this fact is affirmed by the announcement of Major General Fidel Ramos, Chief of the Philippine Constabulary which was published in the August 6, 1977 issue of the "Bulletin Today", copy of which is attached to this traversal as Annex E;

b. Benigno S. Aquino, Jr. is now prosecuted for alleged illegal possession of firearms although he was not found to be in actual physical possession of any firearms, yet Dominador Lacson in whose possession said firearms were seized by the military authorities has never been indicted for the said offense.

c. Benigno S. Aquino, Jr. is now prosecuted for illegal possession of firearms which he could have surrendered without incurring liability under existing Presidential Decrees, yet it was physically and legally impossible for him to do so even if he had firearms in his possession because he was already detained by military authorities as early as September 23, 1977.

d. Benigno S. Aquino, Jr. is now being prosecuted for alleged illegal possession of firearms although none were found in his possession, yet Ali Dimaporo whom the government admitted as having firearms in his possession when martial law was declared is now allowed to sit as head of the "Batasang Panglalawigan" and of the Provisional Government in Muslim provinces.

38. That the denial of the equal protection of the laws, as above described, becomes more palpable and glaring considering the notorious fact, which is of public knowledge and capable of instant and unquestionable demonstration, that the heads of the 145 private armies that had been dismantled at the very start of martial law have not been charged or prosecuted before any military tribunal or any civil court; in point of fact, some of these heads — obviously close to those in power — are now occupying high positions in the martial law Government.

39. That the denial of the equal protection of the laws, as above described, is equally palpable and glaring considering the repeated claim of the martial law government, which are of public knowledge and capable of instant demonstration, that more than 600,000 loose firearms have been confiscated and seized by the military authorities since the start of martial law, that none of the owners of these loose firearms have been charged or prosecuted before any military tribunal or any civil court; worse, accused Benigno S. Aquino, Jr. who was arrested and detained even before the public proclamation of martial law, is being prosecuted for alleged violation of General Order Nos. 6 and 7, in relation to Presidential Decree No. 9 (illegal possession of firearms, explosives and accessories) which were issued and promulgated after his arrest, in violation of the constitutional

guarantee against ex post facto law.

40. That Benigno S. Aquino, Jr. has been detained unlawfully under custody of respondent commission continuously from September 21, 1972 up to the date of filing of this petition for habeas corpus, a total detention period of almost FIVE YEARS and notwithstanding such unconscionable detention, respondent Military Commission has insisted on retaining responsibility for the trial of Benigno S. Aquino, Jr., at variance with what said respondent commission and other military courts have done in the 3,146 cases cited in paragraph 15 of this petition, and such insistence has operated to deny said Benigno S. Aquino, Jr. the equal protection of the laws.

41. That considering the publicly announced return of the country to normalcy, there is no remaining justification for the continued assertion of military courts, particularly respondent Military Commission No. 2 to try civilians like Benigno S. Aquino, Jr. for acts allegedly committed by him before said commission, which exists for the principal purpose of administering justice among persons in the military service; Benigno S. Aquino, Jr. is still detained by respondent when there is no national emergency nor threat to the ability of the civil courts to administer justice in the manner provided by the Philippine Constitution, as claimed by the President of the Philippines and quoted in the *Daily Bulletin,* issue of August 28, 1977, copy of which is hereto attached as Annex "E" and which is exerpted as follows:

> "The President, noting that conditions now merit normalization of the democratic process, said "crime is on the wane, the rebellion has been met, and most important, the way to the eradication of the root causes of crime and insurgency has been effectively made a part of the national life and effort."

> "He added that the economy has attained resiliency and vigorous growth and the country has come to better terms with the rest of the world."

41(a). That the scandalous lack of continuity of membership of the respondent Military Commission No. 2 as starkly presented in the following enumeration of the officers who have sat in the commission since the time the charges against Benigno S. Aquino, Jr. were filed before it precludes the respondent commission from performing its functions in a judicious and deliberate manner because its new members have not informed themselves of the nature of past proceedings which now reach at least 6,000 pages of recorded testimony:

NAME	DATE ASSIGNED
Brig. Gen. Jose G. Syjuco 0-5515 AFP	- detailed President of MC-2 per GO M-2 dtd. 2 Oct. 72

Col. Salvador S. Sardalla
0-4151 JAGS (GSC)

- detailed law member
of MC-2 per GO M-2
dtd. 2 Oct. 72

Col. Jose O. Tansingco
0-3141 PA (GSC)

- detailed member of
MC-2 per GO M-2
dtd. 9 July 73

- relieved as member
of MC-2 per GO M-10
dtd. 16 Sept. 74

Col. Gualberto Miranda
0-28049 PAF (GSC)

- detailed as member
of MC-2 eff. 22
Jan. 73 per GO M-18
dtd. 22. Jan. 73

- relieved as member
of MC-2 per GO
M-29 dtd. 13 Nov. 73

Col. Miguel R. Gantuangco
0-3330 PC (GSC)

- detailed as member
of MC-2 eff. 29 Nov.
72 per GO M-9 dtd.
6 Dec. 72

- relieved as member
of MC-2 eff. as of
24 Sept. 74 per GO
M-50 dtd. 2 Mar. 75

Col. Eduardo A. Arciaga
0-3282 PA (GSC)

- detailed as member
of MC-2 per GO M-36
eff. 1 June 73 dtd.
31 May 73

- relieved as member
of MC-2 per GO M-71
dtd. 22 June 74

Col. Marcelo S. Nuguid
0-3281 PA (GSC)

- detailed as member
of MC-2 per GO M-2
dtd. 9 July 73

- relieved as member
of MC-2 per GO M-3
dtd. 16 July 74

Lt. Col. Leon O. Rosales
0-84414 PA (GSC)

- detailed as member
of MC-2 per GO M-2
dtd. 9 July 73

Capt. Honorio Capulong
0-6228 JAGS (GHQ)

- detailed as
TC of MC-2 per GO M-2
dtd. 9 July 73

Fiscal Pascual Kliatchko

- detailed as Co-Trial
Counsel of MC-2 per
GO M-2 dtd. 9 July 73

Capt. Apolinario Florencio
0-85897 JAGS (PC)

- detailed as Defense
Counsel of MC-2 per
GO M-2 dtd. 9 July 73

- relieved defense
counsel of MC-2
eff. 1 Apr 75
per GO M-48 dtd.
20 March 75

1st Lt. Silverio Taloma
0-102048 JAGS (PAF)

- detailed as Defense
Counsel of MC-2 per
GO M-2 dtd. 9 July 73

- relieved as defense
Counsel of MC-2 per
GO M-59 dtd. 6 May 75

Cmdr. Marciano I. Bacalla
0-4873 JAGS (PN)

- detailed as Special
Law Member of MC-2
per Office Orders
No. 140 dtd. 29 Aug.
77 eff. as of 25 Aug. 77

Capt. Benjamin B. Facto
0-3917 PN (GSC)

- detailed as member
of MC-2 eff. 19 Mar
75 per GO M-48 dtd.
20 March 75

Col. Vicente Yumul
0-3158 PC (GSC)

- detailed as member
of MC-2 per GO M-3
dtd. 17 July 75 eff.
as of 16 July 75

- relieved as member
of MC-2 per GO M-62
dtd. 2 July 76 eff.
upon term of cases
etc.

Col. Timoteo L. Tan
0-4435 PAF

- detailed member of
MC-2 per GO M-30
dtd. 13 Nov. 73

- relieved as member
of MC-2 per GO M-3
dtd. 16 July 74

1st Lt. Dante V. Gil
0-6502 JAGS (GHQ)

- detailed Asst.
Trial Counsel of
MC-2 per GO M-34
dtd. 26 Nov. 73

- relieved as Asst.
TC of MC-2 per GO
M-9 dtd. 23 Aug. 74

Col. Lorenzo C. Villaflor
0-3797 PA (GSC)

- detailed as member
of MC-2 per GO-M3
dtd. 16 July 74

- relieved as member
of MC-2 per GO M-34
dtd. 7 Feb. 75

Col. Urbano C. Espinosa
0-81189 PA (GSC)

- detailed as member
of MC-2 per GO
M-10 dtd. 16 Sept. 74

- relieved as member
of MC-2 per GO
M-63 dtd. 20 June 75

1st Lt. Orlando D. Beltran
0-6638 JAGS (GHQ)

- detailed as Co-Trial
Counsel of MC-2 per
GO M-17 dtd. 17 Oct.
74 eff. 3 Oct. 74

- relieved as Co-Trial
Counsel of MC-2 per
GO M-16 dtd. 15
Sept. 75 eff. as of 10
Sept. 75

Lt. Col. German Atienza — detailed as member — name cancelled
0-4325 PA   of MC-2 per GO M-34   from GO M-34 per
                          dtd. 7 Feb. eff. 16   GO M-42 dtd. 10
                          Feb. 75   March 75

Col. Stefani C. Domingo — detailed as member — relieved as member
0-3476 PC (GSC)   of MC-2 eff. 21 Mar. of MC-2 per GO M-3
                          75 per GO M-50 dtd.   dtd. 17 July 75
                          21 March 75   eff. upon term of
                                                cases, etc.

Col. Emifrio Torres — detailed as member — name is nullified
0-3271 PA (GSC)   of MC-2 per GO M-64   from GO M-64 as
                      dtd. 20 June 75 eff. member of MC-2 per
                      1 July 75   GO M-13 dtd. 28
                                            Aug. 75

Capt. Antonio B. Manzano — detailed as Defense — relieved as Defense
0-105313 JAGS (PC)   Counsel of MC-2 per   Counsel of MC-2 per
                           GO M-35 dtd. 23   GO M-30 dtd. 12
                           June 73 eff. as of   June 76 eff. as of 6
                           15 June 75   Jan. 76

1st Lt. Vicente M. Tagoc, Jr. — detailed as Co-Defense
0-105322 JAGS (PC)   Counsel of MC-2 per GO
                               M-56 dtd. 23 Apr. 75
                               eff. as of 20 Apr. 75

Col. Antonio V. Achurra — detailed as member of
0-36354 (GSC) MNSU   MC-2 per GO M-65 dtd.
                         26 Jul 76 eff. as of
                         21 June 76

Lt. Col. Doroteo Coronel — detailed as member of
0-4007 PAF   MC-2 per GO M-62 dtd.
                         2 July 76 eff. as of
                         15 Jul 76

Col. Ernesto L. Macadaeg — detailed as member of
0-3453 PA (GSC)   MC-2 per GO M-1 dtd.
                         1 July 75 eff. as of
                         1 July 75

Col. Gabriel A. Victoria 0-4412 PAF (GSC)	- detailed as member of MC-2 per GO M-8 dtd. 31 July 75 eff. as of 1 August 75
Fiscal Macario Galang	- detailed Co-Trial Counsel in PP vs. Benigno S. Aquino, Jr. et al. per office orders No. 126 dtd. 13 Aug. 76
Lt. Col. Juan Sison 0-104814 JAGS (PC)	- detailed Trial Coun- sel of MC-2 per of- fice orders No. 109 dtd. 16 July 76
1st Lt. Pablito dela Cruz 0-6639 JAGS (GHQ)	- detailed as Co-Trial Counsel in PP vs. Be- nigno S. Aquino, Jr. et al. per Office Orders No. 103 eff. 15 July 76
Lt. Col. Gonzalo T. Santos 0-105749 JAGS (GSC)	- detailed as Defense Counsel in PP vs. Be- nigno S. Aquino, Jr. et al. per Office Orders No. 109 dtd. 16 July 76
Maj. Percival G. Pasion 0-6135 JAGS (GHQ)	- detailed as Co-Defense Counsel in PP vs. Benigno S. Aquino, Jr., et al. per Office Orders No. 103 dtd. 13 July 76 eff. 15 July 76

Of the original members of the Commission, only its President, Brig. Gen. Jose Syjuco, sits in the Commission. Old members have been replaced and new members have come in without having the opportunity to study antecedent records and proceedings because the said proceedings were not promptly transcribed by the stenographers. It is quite obvious that had it been the pleasure of the Commander-in-Chief of the Armed Forces to insure continuity of the members of the Commission, such safeguards could have been taken without disrupting the smooth functioning of the entire military establishment. Retiring officers who were members of the commission could have been extended in their tours of duty as has been done with respect to General Syjuco, but this was never applied with respect to the other members of the Commission. All of these lapses give strong reason to believe that the proceedings before the respondent commissions are not impartial, contrary to the standard clearly stated in the Universal Declaration of Human Rights. One of the features of a fair trial is that the judge or the members of the tribunal have ample opportunity to observe the demeanor of the witnesses who appear before them in order that they can form their impressions about the candor or mendacity of said witnesses, but this salutary feature has been lost entirely under the system of unexpired changes in the composition of the military commission.

42. That the capricious insistence of respondent Military Commission No. 2 in asserting its sole responsibility for trial of the charges which have been filed against Benigno S. Aquino, Jr. who is not a member of the military establishment cannot find support in a country like the Philippines which is claimed to adhere to constitutionalism nor in a country like the Philippines whose adherence to respect for human rights has been characterized by the President of the Philippines as "irrevocable".

43. The right of Petitioner to invoke the writ of habeas corpus to obtain the release of her son who has been deprived of the equal protection of the laws was not foreclosed in Aquino vs. Enrile, L-37364 because:

a. The issue which was resolved in the cited case was the authority of military courts to try civilians at the inception of martial law, unlike the issue which is now before this Honorable Supreme Court which refers to the continued exercise of that power by military courts five years after the proclamation of martial law under present conditions which have been described by the President of the Philippines as "the independence and inviolability of the civil courts have been sustained and even enhanced under Martial law".

b. The recognition of authority of the President to proclaim martial law in the Philippines and to create military tribunals has not validated any and all acts of the subordinates of the President, or even those of the President himself, when such acts, as in the case at bar, deprive Benigno S. Aquino, Jr. of the equal protection of the laws in the light of the environment under which civil courts function today. On this point, Justice Barredo's separate concurring opinion concurring against any sweeping extension of the doctrine in said case to other cases is very emphatic, to wit:

"This decision that could well be *sui generis,* hence, whatever has been said here would necessarily govern questions related to adverse claims of authority related to the lower levels of hierarchy of powers in the Constitution."

Aquino, Jr., et al. vs
Enrile, etc., et al.,
Supreme Court Decisions,
September 1974, p. 520)

c. The decision of the Supreme Court in the cited case is not resjudicata on the present petition because the cause of action in the present petition can be distinguished from the cause of action in the former case.

d. The cited case L-37364 is a mere decision which can be overturned in the light of the political realities today distinguished from the political realities when said decision was promulgated, and it is submitted that a compelling rational basis exists today for departing from said ruling.

44. Petitioner submits that the following circumstances under which Benigno S. Aquino, Jr. will be tried by respondent commission, taken together, have ousted the said commission of its jurisdiction over Benigno S. Aquino, Jr. and over the offenses charged against him:

a. The said proceedings are void because the President of the Philippines and his representatives do not have judicial power under the Constitution, although the President and his representatives may exercise both legislative and executive power during the emergency under martial law:

b. The said proceedings are void because the presidential decrees and the general orders under which Benigno S. Aquino, Jr. is being prosecuted are in the nature of ex post facto legislation.

c. The said proceedings are void because leaders and followers who have risen in arms against the government and who have killed a big number of government troops in open combat have been pampered, benefited and rewarded while Benigno S. Aquino, Jr. is singled out for indictment and public humiliation.

d. The said proceedings are void because Benigno S. Aquino, Jr. has been deprived of the benefits of the ruling in People vs. Hernandez which is now part of the law of the land.

e. The said proceedings are void because for purposes of avoiding the Hernandez ruling the military commission has treated the allegation of murder against the accused as a common crime which is not absorbed in the offense of subversion, yet for purposes of justifying its own jurisdiction the same is treated as a political offense that affects national security.

45. That the posture of the Philippines as a country which does not pay mere lip service to the protection of human rights has been rendered incredible by the insistence of respondent Military Commission No. 2 to assume the responsibility for the trial of civilian Benigno S. Aquino, Jr., and the injury to the personal dignity

of Benigno S. Aquino, Jr., arising from such discrimination and denial of the equal protection of the laws has become inestimable.

46. That the issuance of the writ of habeas corpus for the unconditional release of Benigno S. Aquino, Jr. from his unlawful detention by respondent Military Commission No. 2 will complement the statement of the President of the Philippines in an article entitled "Martial Law and Human Rights" which was distributed to the delegates to the recently concluded Manila World Law Conference, and which is quoted below:

> "The constitutional safeguards that are meant to protect the independence and inviolability of the civil courts have been sustained and even enhanced under Martial law."

47. That Petitioner has no other recourse in the ordinary course of law to obtain the release of Benigno S. Aquino, Jr. from the unlawful detention by respondent Military Commission No. 2 notwithstanding the fact that said Benigno S. Aquino, Jr. has been flagrantly denied the equal protection of the laws except by filing the present petition for habeas corpus, the most important and most immediately available safeguard of his liberty, and invoking the constitutional and equitable powers of the Honorable Supreme Court in whose hands the rule of law in this country is expected to become alive and meaningful.

48. That respondent Military Commission No. 2 is about to try Petitioner's son Benigno S. Aquino, Jr. on December 5, 1977, and unless restrained by means of a writ of preliminary injunction ex parte or by means of a temporary restraining order, said respondent will proceed without jurisdiction or in excess of its jurisdiction, causing irreparable injury to Petitioner and to her son Benigno S. Aquino, Jr.

49. That Petitioner is entitled to the relief demanded in this petition for habeas corpus, and that such relief consists in obtaining the release of Benigno S. Aquino, Jr. from unlawful restraint and preventing the Respondent Commission from acting without or in excess of its jurisdiction.

50. That Petitioner is ready to file a bond in any reasonable amount which may be set by this Honorable Supreme Court which shall be answerable for any damage or prejudice which may be suffered by the respondent arising from the issuance of the writ of preliminary injunction or temporary restraining order which may be issued by the Honorable Supreme Court as herein prayed for.

WHEREFORE, premises considered, it is respectfully prayed that upon receipt of this Petition, a writ of habeas corpus be issued requiring the immediate production by the respondent Military Commission No. 2, Secretary of National Defense and the Chief of Staff, Armed Forces of the Philippines of the body of

Benigno S. Aquino, Jr. before the Honorable Supreme Court on a date which it may specify, that a writ of preliminary injunction and or temporary restraining order be issued ex parte preventing the Respondent Commission from proceeding with the trial of Benigno S. Aquino, Jr. on December 5, 1977, and that after trial or hearing, the release of said Benigno S. Aquino, Jr. from the unlawful detention by said respondent Military Commission No. 2 be ordered because he has been denied the equal protection of the laws, because he will twice be put in jeopardy, and because the essence of decent life has been taken away from him without due process of law; with costs against the Respondents.

Makati, Metro Manila for the City of Manila, 2 December, 1977.

SALONGA, ORDOÑEZ, YAP & ASSOCIATES
Suite 322-327 Rufino Building
Ayala Avenue, Makati
Metro Manila

- and -

RAÙL M. GONZALES
Room 607 May Building
Rizal Avenue, Manila
Counsel for Petitioner

By:

SEDFREY A. ORDOÑEZ

RAUL M. GONZALES

Copy Furnished:

Solicitor General
Manila, Counsel for Respondent

VERIFICATION

I, AURORA A. AQUINO, of legal age, hereby depose and say:

That I am the Petitioner in the above entitled case;

That I have caused the preparation of the foregoing Supplemental Petition for Habeas Corpus;

That I have read the contents thereof and that the allegations therein are true and correct of my own knowledge.

AURORA A. AQUINO

SUBSCRIBED AND SWORN to before me this 3rd day of December, 1977 affiant exhibited to me her Residence Certificate No. A-3895085 issued at Concepcion, Tarlac, on April 11, 1977.

DALMACIO A. DY BUCO III
NOTARY PUBLIC
Until December 31, 1977
PTR No.
Makati, Metro Manila
January 20, 1977

DOC. NO. 30
PAGE NO. 7
BOOK NO. III
SERIES OF 1977.

INDEX

Index